Map of the Taw-Torridge estuary showing Appledore, Instow, Braunton Sand, Horsey Island, Yelland, Sprat Ridge and surrounding areas.

BRAUNTON
HOME OF THE LAST SAILING COASTERS

Robert D'Arcy Andrew MBE

LOTTERY FUNDED

PUBLISHED BY BRAUNTON & DISTRICT MUSEUM,
THE BAKEHOUSE CENTRE, CAEN STREET, BRAUNTON, NORTH DEVON EX33 2ED

© Robert D'Arcy Andrew MBE and various authors 2007

All rights reserved. No part of this publication may be reproduced, stored in a retrieval system or transmitted in any form by any means electrical, mechanical or otherwise without first seeking the permission of the publisher.

THE BRITISH LIBRARY CATALOGUING IN PUBLICATION DATA:
A CATALOGUE RECORD FOR THIS BOOK IS AVAILABLE FROM THE BRITISH LIBRARY

ISBN: 978-1-902310-04-6

PRINTED BY WESTPRINT, CLYST St. MARY, EXETER EX5 1SA   TEL: 01395 233 442

To Michael

With compliments and best wishes

from

Cecil

THE BRAUNTON AND DISTRICT MUSEUM

REGISTERED CHARITY NO: 1010422

OFFICERS:

President	John Bury
Chairman	Roy Lucas
Vice Chairman	Robert D'Arcy Andrew
Administrator	Jackie Edwards
Treasurer	David Hook
Trustees:	Ray Copper, Jeff Miles, Les Squance

All correspondence relating to membership, offers of assistance and meetings, should be sent to the Administrator at:-

Braunton & District Museum, The Bakehouse Centre, Caen Street, Braunton, North Devon EX33 2ED
Tel: 01271 816 688
www.devonmuseums.net/braunton

The Annual Subscription is a minimum of £5.00 per person payable by Bank Standing Order, or to the Administrator, address as above. Wherever possible we would prefer that this is by means of "Gift Aid" as this benefits the Museum. Life Membership is also available from £25.00. Full details are available from the Administrator, Jackie Edwards.

Front Cover: A painting of the "Result" as she appeared in 'Outcast of the Isles' by C. Keith Andrew

CONTENTS:

List of illustrations

Introduction

1. Braunton – Home of the last Sailing Coasters   1
    Peter Thomson

2. Life and Times   17
    Robert D'Arcy Andrew

3. The story of *Result*   31
    Tom Welch

4. The sand and gravel trade   45
    David Clement and Robert D'Arcy Andrew

5. Approaching the Bar   59
    Robert D'Arcy Andrew

6. Wreck and Rescue   67
    David Clement

7. Mariners of Braunton   79
    The late Stan Rogers and David Clement

8. The Pierhead Paintings   91
    David Clement

9. Schedule of Braunton owned vessels   119

    Gravel Barges   222

    Addendum   222

Additional Addendum

Braunton Home of the Last Sailing Coasters

Final disposal of vessels
not recorded in the schedule

Amy	Scuttled for film 1928
Ann	Hulked Swansea 1942
Charlotte	Broken up 1929
Daring	Broken up 1929
Dispatch	Foundered off Combe Martin 1912
Eliza Anne	Sunk by U-boat off Lizard 1918
Elizabeth (15324)	Broken up 1906
Henrietta	Hulked 1907
Honour	Wrecked Skomer 1911
Margaret	Converted to motorised salvage vessel 1917
Mary	Hulked 1925
Priory	Broken up after collision Guernsey 1919
Olive Branch	Broken up Appledore 1947
Stranger	Broken up 1924
Vision	Missing 1921
Why Not	Hulked 1911

ILLUSTRATIONS

No.		Page
	Chart showing the entrance over the Bar	Inside front
	From a chart of Barnstaple & Bideford surveyed by Cdr. G. M. Alldridge, Mr. D. Hall, master and W. Quinn, RN, 1855 with small corrections to 1908.	
	Map of Braunton waterway by S. Ellacott	FP 1

Chapter 1 Home of the last fleet of sailing coasters

1	The gravel barge "*Hilda*", with the ketches "*Ann*" and "*Bessie*" at Braunton	2
2	The ketch "*Lewisman*" and the "*Maude*", lying in Braunton Pill	3
3	The ketch "*Bessie*" unloading coal at Velator	4
4	The steel schooner "*Result*" and the wooden ketch "*Bessie*" at Velator 1939	5
5	The ketch "*Ann*" and the ketch "*Bessie*" at Velator with Tom Slee, on the bank with a bag and John (Jan 'Bull') Mitchell in the ship's boat	6
6	The smack "*Hilda*" unloading gravel at Velator taken from the Bar. The ketch "*Bessie*" lying behind.	7
7	The ketches "*Acacia*", "*Lizza*", "*Murray*" and "*Bonita*" in Appledore Pool	8
8	The "*C.F.H.*" lying at Velator	9
9	The ketch "*Enid*" lying at Velator Quay	10
10	The "*Acacia*" and the "*Crown of Denmark*" at Big Quay.	11
11	"*Maud Mary*", the ketch "*Thomas*" and the "*Trio*" off Appledore	12
12	Braunds, the local sailmakers	13
13	The "*St. Austell*" and "*Maud*" of Bideford at Braunton Quay 13 Sept. 1946.	14
14	Velator Quay, with from left to right, the "*Result*" as a 3-masted schooner, ketch "*Democrat*", the sailing gravel barge "*Hilda*" and the former sailing barge "*Rowena*" with the hull of the schooner "*Elsie*" behind, being broken up.	15

Chapter 2 Life and times

15	Robert's boat "*Salar*" ready for launching in 1945, with friends and family celebrating the occasion	18
16	The "*Salar*", unrigged, at Velator, showing the quayside opposite, off which lies the small seaweed barge "*Dorothy*".	18
17	"*Salar*" at sea with Captain Steve Chugg enjoying a trip on Robert's boat.	18
18	The young boatbuilder, aged 17 with Pamela Fowler – the girl next door – and her brother Leonard, aboard "*Salar*" at the Bar buoy at dead low water.	18
19	The ketch "*Enid*" at Velator, 1947	19
20	"*Result*" drying her sails at Ilfracombe, about 1951	20
21	The small seaweed barge "*Dorothy*"	22
22	"*Result*" entering Turf Lock, Exeter Canal around 1930 after delivering a cargo of cement	23
23	"*Result*" when filming as "Flash" in 1950, with (left to right) Sid Crick, Mickey Kemp, Sam Mitchell, Peter Welch and Robert Andrew.	24
24	"*Result*" when filming in 1950 as "Flash" in "Outcast of the Islands" seen in the Isles of Scilly	25
25	The ss "*Farringay*" seen under the port quarter of the "*Result*" at Appledore	28
26	"*Result*" in New Quay dry dock, June 1952 with Robert Andrew under her bows having completed tarring the hull with Sam Mitchell	30

No.		Page
	Chapter 3 the story of the "Result"	
27	"*Result*" as a topsail schooner in 1895	31
28	"*Result* at Pill's Mouth, Velator Creek as a topsail schooner	32
29	"*Result*" as HMS "Q23"	33
30	"*Result*" – her record as a "Q" ship in 1917	33
31	The Bill of Sale for 16 shares in the "*Result*" which were transferred from Susan Incledon, the wife of Captain Incledon, to Francis Ann Welch the wife of the ship's master on 25 June 1923 for £600.	34
32	"*Result*" off Beachy Head in 1922 laden with Portmadoc slate bound for Amsterdam.	34
33	"*Result*" seen light at Velator at the top of a spring tide pre-1939. One can see the top of a pile of gravel on the quayside where a gravel barge has just completed discharging.	35
34	"*Result*" at Asham, 1936	36
35	"*Result*" lying in Ilfracombe in 1952	36
36	"*Result*" at Jersey in the late 1950s	37
37	"*Result*" when filming in 1950 as "Flash" in "Outcast of the Islands" seen in the Isles of Scilly.	37
38	The "*Result*" as the schooner "*Flash*", when filming "The Outcast of the Islands"	38
39	"Ketch "*Garlandstone*" and "*Result*" at Big Quay, Velator	39
40	The 3-masted schooner "*Result*" leaving Solva	40
41	"*Result*" leaving Solva, rounding St. David's Head	40
42	An insurance certificate for the "*Result*"	41
43	"*Result*" as a topsail schooner, at Stanbury's Mill, Barnstaple.	42
44	Early 1960s, "*Result*" now a two-masted ketch, discharging coal, at Tresco, Isles of Scilly.	42
45	"*Result*" rounding Land's End	43
46	The mv "*Polar Bear*" supply ship to Lundy Island	44
47	The crew of the "*Result*" about 1936: Peter Welch, Tom Welch, 'Smuggler' Hall and Peter Russan	44
	Chapter 4 The Sand and gravel trade	
48	Sailing barges loading in the early 1900s.	45
49	A wintry scene with two barges passing down the river Taw from Barnstaple to collect gravel in the early years of the 20th. century	46
50	Barges off Appledore Quay and waiting to go at 8.30am., June 2 1954 - seen from the deck of "*Flower*" are left to right, "*Result*", "*Paul & Michael*", the ketch "*Maud Mary*", with the "*Princess Maysie*" just visible in front, and the "*Julie Pile*" alongside to starboard.	47
51	Bound out – "*Result*" and the barge "*Paul and Michael*"	47
52	Barges at Klondike, near Bideford Bar preparing to anchor, left to right "Result with the grab, the "*Flower*", "*A.C.M.*" and the "*Julie Pile*" in June 1954.	48
53	Anchors down and waiting to dry out on the gravel banks 2 June 1954 – left to right, "*Marie*", " and "*Result*" seen from the deck of the "*Nellie*"	48
54	Barges loading – with "*Paul & Michael*", "*Julie Pile*", and the "*Flower*"	50
55	Barges loading at Klondike, June 1954, with "*ACM*", "*Result*," "*Paul & Michael*" the "*Julie Pile*" and beyond "the "*Princess Mayse*".	50

No.		Page
56	Looking from Klondike, towards Appledore from the "*Nellie*" with "*Julie Pile*", "*Flower*", "*Paul & Michael*" and "*Rowena*" in the distance, with the "*ACM*" on the right.	51
57	Flood tide coming in with "*Julie Pile*", "*Flower*", "*Paul & Michael*", "*Rowena*" and "*ACM*" seen from aboard "Nellie" with the crew of the latter getting in the anchor.	52
58	Almost Afloat – with "*Nellie*", "*PKH*", "*Result*", with the dinghy of the "*Flower*" in the foreground	52
59	Waiting to float off – aboard the "*Nellie*", with the "*Julie Pile*", and the "*Paul & Michael*" ahead.	53
60	Getting afloat – "*Princess Mayse*" with her Bartletts grab crane, and the "*Result*".	54
61	Returning with the "*Maud Mary*", "*Paul & Michael*" and "*Princess Mayse*"	54
62	Deep laden, the "*Paul & Michael*" returns	55
63	The barge "*Marie*" of Salcombe, now a gravel barge returning up the Torridge with sand in May 1951	55
64	Gravel being unloaded from the sailing barge "*Hilda*" at Braunton Pill, with the quayside awash.	56
65	Four barges discharging at Braunton – including the sailing barge "*Hilda*" in August 1943. The timber baffles on the quayside that prevented the hard-won cargo from being washed back into the channel at the top of the tide, can be clearly seen	56
66	Loading in the 1940s – "*ACM*" and "*Advance*" off Crow Point	58

Chapter 5 Approaching the Bar

67	Braunton Higher Light showing sailing vessels beating out over the Bar.	60
68	The Higher Light showing the half-tide mark directly in front on the foreshore.	61
69	A fine aerial photograph of the High Light looking across the estuary towards Westward Ho!	61
70	Braunton Low Light showing the Tide Ball alongside with the two pulley wires to enable this to be raised when required.	62
71	"Blinking Billy" – The Bideford Bar Lighthouse.	64
72	The remains of "Blinking Billy", erected in 1908 and altered in 1920.	65
73	Braunton Higher Light. The Tide Ball, which was raised on a pulley when it was safe to cross the Bar, can be seen to the left of the Lighthouse.	66

Chapter 6 Wreck and rescue

74	The iron ship "*Penthesilea*" of Liverpool lying at Fowey. She was wrecked on North Tail, Braunton January 1890 carrying coal	72
75	Braunton lifeboat photographed around 1890	74
76	The occasion in 1902 when Braunton took delivery of its new lifeboat	74
77	The wreck of the "*Phyllis Grey*" thrown on Saunton Sands 9 Sept. 1908.	75
78	Braunton Life Boat house in the early 1900s with the lifeboat "*Robert & Catherine*" ready for service.	75
79	Braunton Lifeboat "*Robert & Catherine*" launching.	76
80	Recovering the lifeboat	77
81	The topsail schooner "*Volant*" ashore on Saunton Sands, Easter Thursday 1917	78
82	An unknown wreck uncovered on Saunton Sands – February 2005	78

No.		Page
	Chapter 7 The Mariners of Braunton	
83	Certificate of competency – Captain George Chugg, 1868	84
84	Thomas Clarke, John Mitchell and John Clarke – three ninety-year-old ex-masters of Braunton sailing vessels seen in 1934	85
85	Three generations William, Samuel and Frank Mitchell	85
86	Fred Mitchell, Tom Welch, Frank Mitchell and an unknown member of the crew of "*Result*"	85
87	Sam Mitchell	86
88	Bill Mitchell	86
89	The 3-masted ship "*Castleton*"	86
90	The barque "*Claverdon*" in which John Elliott served.	87
91	Len Baglole	87
92	Bill Crocker	87
93	Captain Jack Newcombe aboard "*Eilian*"	88
94	Pilot Thomas Bassett at the helm of the ketch "*Acacia*"	88
95	The ship "*Celtic Chief*"	89
96	Reg Williams and Captain Bob Parkhouse aboard the "*Mary Stewart*"	90
97	Brian Herniman	90
98	Roger Chugg	91
99	Richard Olden	91
100	The "*Garlandstone*", outside Swansea North Dock Basin on Saturday 20 September 1958	91
	Chapter 8 The pierhead paintings	
101	Reuben Chappell, 1870-1940	92
102	The ketch "*Agnes*", seen in her later days complete with a wheelhouse by Mark Myers.	93
103	The ketch "*Annie Christian*", when she was owned in Watchet, later the Braunton "*Ade*", painted by J. H. Harrison of Swansea.	94
104	The ketch "*Bessie Clark*", owned by George Clark of Braunton by an unknown artist	95
105	A fine photograph of the "*Bessie Ellen*" powering along and now fully restored by Nicki Alford by Jon Seagrave	96
106	"*Bessie Ellen*" practically becalmed in 2006. Photograph by Jon Seagrave.	97
107	The ketch "*Daring*" built in 1863 at Bideford, Captain Frank Mitchell of Braunton, painted by Reuben Chappell.	98
108	A rough weather portrait of the schooner "*Eilian*" by Reuben Chappell	99
109	The fine weather painting by Reuben Chappell, showing the schooner "*Eilian*" under full sail.	100
110	A fine painting by Reuben Chappell of the ketch "*Four Brothers*"	101
111	A 'rough' weather scene of the ketch "*Four Brothers*" painted by Reuben Chappell	102
112	An Italian pierhead painter's view of the "*John Blackwell*" of Bideford, entering Naples in December 1864	103
113	The ketch "*Julie*" of Malpas, owned in her final days by the artist's father and painted by Eric Voysey of Topsham.	104
114	The ketch "*Lenora*", owned by the Chichester family of Braunton from 1884 until she was wrecked in 1913, painted by J. H. Harrison	105
115	The schooner "*Morning Star*", Captain S. Corney, painted by Reuben Chappell	106

No.		Page
116	The ketch "*Olive Branch*", painted by Reuben Chappell.	107
117	The ketch "*Pirate*" of Barnstaple, owned by the Drake family for most of her working life, believed to be by J. H. Harrison	108
118	The ketch "*Priory*" owned for most of her long life by the Incledon family of Braunton, believed to be by J. H. Harrison.	109
119	The schooner "*Result*" in her earlier days, painted by Reuben Chappell	110
120	A fine painting by Reuben Chappell, of the "*Result*" as a three masted fore-and-aft schooner.	111
121	The second of the pair of Reuben Chappell paintings of the "*Result*" showing her in rough weather.	112
122	The ketch "*Rosie*", built by Robert Cock at Appledore, seen in her later days, painted by Reuben Chappell	113
123	The schooner "*Rosie*" of Appledore as originally built by Robert Cock, painted by Reuben Chappell	114
124	The ketch "*St. Austell*", painted by local artist Brian Bale.	115
125	The schooner "*Waterlily*" owned by the Chugg family of Braunton from 1910, painted by Reuben Chappell.	116
126	Braunton Pill showing the position of the moorings of the last 25 sailing coasters trading from there.	117
127	Velator today with Big Quay, the slipway where cargoes of seaweed were unloaded, and Little Quay, now a haven for pleasure craft	118

Chapter 9 Braunton Vessels

128	"*Acacia*" beating out of the estuary around 1906, with Braunton Lighthouse behind.	119
129	A spot of tender care - Captain William Rogers and George Dendle tarring the bottom of "*Acacia*" at Appledore in 1906	119
130	"*Acacia*" on the hard at Braunton Pill	120
131	"*Acacia*" – deck scene	120
132	The fine ketch "*Ade*" seen on Appledore beach	121
133	"*Ade*" having discharged a cargo of coal	121
134	The Ketch "*Ade*" leaving Lynmouth in 1934	122
135	"*Agnes*" loading wheat feed at Barry in 1955	122
136	"*Agnes*" loading wheat feed at Barry in 1955	122
137	The ketch "*Agnes*" stranded at Kinsale, Ireland in 1919.	123
138	"*Agnes*" leaving Bude, in 1935 light for Lydney, and another cargo of coal	123
139	The "*Agnes*" sailing inside the Nash Sands	124
140	Porthclain Harbour, St. Davids with the ketch "*Agnes*" discharging.	124
141	The "*Agnes*" discharging at Rolle Quay, Barnstaple 25 August 1949	125
142	"*Agnes*" discharging coal at Bude in 1937	125
143	The "*Alfred & Emma*" seen entering the tiny harbour of Porthgain.	126
144	"*Ann*" of Salcombe, discharging coal from Lydney, at Lynmouth in 1924	127
145	The "*Ann*" of Salcombe, her deep narrow hull seen to advantage at Velator.	128
146	"*Ann*", discharging Lydney coal at Velator	129
147	Cargo handling aboard the "*Ann*" in 1927, discharging sand and gravel.	129
148	Ketch "*Ann*" discharging into a lorry on the beach at Combe Martin	130
149	A moody photograph of the "*Ann*" lying off Appledore, in 1941 when commanded by Captain Jim Screech.	131

No.		Page
150	"*A.T.*" seen at Bude	132
151	"*A.T*", Running free	132
152	The "*Bessie*" lying at Velator, Braunton.	133
153	The deep-laden "*Bessie*" lying outside Sully & Co's premises waiting to leave Lydney with another cargo of coal.	133
154	The "*Bessie*" lying empty at Bude having discharged coal in 1937	134
155	Captain Tom A. Slee 1934	135
156	The "*Bessie Clark*" at Velator	135
157	The *"Bessie Clark"* lying at Porlock waiting to discharge her cargo of coal	135
158	The *"Bessie Clark"* lying at Velator, Braunton waiting for the tide	136
159	Lying at Rolle Quay, Barnstaple outside W. Dalling & Sons' coal stores are the ketches *"Bessie Clark"*, the *"Ocean Gem"* and the *"Lewisman"*.	136
160	"*Bessie Ellen*" lying off Burnham in 1937	137
161	"*Bessie Ellen*" under full sail departing from Ramsey Harbour, 1909	138
162	The crew of *"Bessie Ellen"* in 1920, with Bill Bray, Jack Chichester, John Watt and Reg Williams	139
163	"*Bessie Ellen*" at Bristol in 1911, with John Chichester and Charlie Mitchell	139
164	The *"Bessie Gould"* laden with basic slag in the entrance to Bude on 14 April 1936	140
165	"*Bessie Gould*" loading gravel on Crow Gravel Ridge in 1920	140
166	The ketch "*Bonita*" sailing past Instow off Appledore	141
167	A dramatic photograph showing the loss of the ketch "*Bonita*" near Barry, South Wales on 1 August 1934	142
168	The "*C.F.H.*" seen at Penarth in 1939	143
169	The crew of "*C.F.H.*" seen at Velator around 1930.	143
170	Ilfracombe before the 1939/45 War with the three-masted schooner "*M. A. James*" in the foreground and the ketch "*C.F.H.*" lying behind.	144
171	The "*Clara May*" at Pill, 1939	145
172	The "*Clara May*" lying at Velator	146
173	"*Clara May*" approaching Bude, 1910	146
174	The "*Clara May*" off Appledore, about 1935, Captain Alf Parkhouse	147
175	The steel motor ketch "*Crown of Denmark*" at sea	147
176	The ketch "*Daring*" at Appledore about 1922	148
177	The ketch "*Democrat*" ghosts along through Milford Haven	149
178	"*Democrat*" in Velator Pool	150
179	"*Democrat*" lying in Bude Canal	150
180	A busy scene at Rolle Quay, Barnstaple, with the ketches "*Democrat*", "*Enid*", Mary Stewart", "*Bessie*", "*Ocean Gem*" and "*Maude*" outside Stanbury's Mills	151
181	The auxiliary ketch "*Dido C.*" at Velator Quay, in 1939.	152
182	The auxiliary ketch "*Dido C.*" at Velator Quay, in 1939.	152
183	"*Dido C.*" discharging coal on Bryher, Isles of Scilly about 1930	152
184	The "*Dido C.*" grounded on the Morte Stone, in 1936.	153
185	The schooner "*Eilian*" lying in Ilfracombe	155
186	Under full sail, the "*Eilian*" makes a fine picture	155
187	In an almost dead calm, the schooner "*Eilian*", deep laden with coal for the local gasworks, enters Ilfracombe	156
188	A lovely photograph which shows the lines of the "*Eilian*" to perfection.	157
189	The ketch "*Elizabeth*" seen about 1914	158
190	The remains of the "*Elsie*" broken up at Velator in the 1920s	159
191	The "*Emily Barratt*" at Ilfracombe, 1938	160

No.		Page
192	*"Emily Barrett"* entering the refurbished Sea Lock at the entrance to Bude in 1960.	161
193	*"Emma Louise"* showing the deck layout of an auxiliary ketch of the 1920s.	162
194	Loaded down to her marks the *"Emma Louise"* delivers another cargo.	162
195	*"Emma Louise"* lying at Appledore in 1953	163
196	*"Enid"* sailing off the Valley of the Rocks, Lynton in 1937, possibly deep laden with gravel.	163
197	*"Enid"* lying at Velator in 1947	164
198	*"Enid"* sailing light in the Bristol Channel in 1939, from the ketch *"Clara May"*	164
199	The *"Enid"* at Neath, South Wales, unloading a cargo of gravel	165
200	The ketch *"Enid"* at Velator Quay	166
201	The ketch *"F.A.M.E."* in Gloucester Docks	166
202	*"F.A.M.E."* lying under Lantern Hill, Ilfracombe at low water	167
203	James Goss' Yard at Calstock in 1909 with *"Garlandstone"* in frame with the Calstock Viaduct being built.	168
204	The completed *"Garlandstone"* ready for launching at Calstock.	169
205	1909 - At the end of her maiden passage *"Garlandstone"* lies proudly off her owner master's home at Musselwick, St. Ishmaels in Dale Roads.	169
206	*"Garlandstone"* working out of Swansea	170
207	The *"Hanna"* at St. Peter Port, Guernsey, laden with lime in 1948	170
208	The *"Hanna"* arriving at Dunball on the river Parrett in 1947	171
209	The *"Hanna"* wrecked at La Corbiére, Jersey in 1949	171
210	The gravel barge *"Hilda"*, the last such vessel to work under sail,	173
211	The little gravel barge *"Hilda,"* light before proceeding to the loading area off Crow Point	173
212	*"Isabel"* proceeding to sea.	175
213	The ketch *"J.M.J."* wrecked on the Isle of Arran	176
214	The *"Julie"* when owned in Topsham sailing on the Exe Estuary	178
215	The *"Kate"*, rigged as a ketch, lying at Ilfracombe with a smack alongside.	179
216	The topsail schooner *"Kate"* under full sail as she was originally rigged	180
217	The *"Kitty Ann"* and the *"Yeo"*, see later, on the gravel banks	180
218	The crew of the *"Kitty Ann"* and the gang of loaders pause under the bows, whilst loading a cargo of gravel from the banks.	181
219	The *"Kitty Ann"* and the *"Mary"* being broken up at Velator about 1925	181
220	The ketch *"Lark"* at Pilton	182
221	Captain Thomas Gideon Bassett and his crew of two aboard the ketch *"Lark"*.	183
222	*"Lewisman"* lying in Braunton Pill	184
223	The ketches *"Lewisman"*, *"Ann"* and *"C.F.H."*	184
224	*"Lewisman"* at Gould's Store, Barnstaple.	185
225	The *"Maggie Annie"* lying off Appledore	186
226	A group of ketches lying in Bude in the early 1900s. The vessel carring the white sail is the *"Margaret"*	187
227	*"Margaret"* leaving Appledore.	188
228	The *"Mary Eliezer"* discharging in Newport, Isle of Wight circa 1940	189
229	The graceful lines of the *"Mary Eliezer"* seen to advantage in Ilfracombe.	189
230	The *"Mary Eliezer"* and a steamship seen together in the Richmond Dry Dock at Appledore.	190
231	The figurehead of the *"Mary Stewart"*	191
232	The *"Mary Stewart"* entering the Cumberland Basin, Bristol, through the lock at Hotwells.	191

No.		Page
233	The *"Mary Stewart"* discharging the last coal cargo to be unloaded at the Big Quay, Velator about 1959.	192
234	The *"Maude"* rigged as a ketch, preparing to leave Appledore	193
235	*"Maude"* alongside Rolle Quay, at Barnstaple.	193
236	*"Morning Star"* of Padstow when rigged as a topsail schooner outside Hawkins coal yard at Padstow about 1900	194
237	Captain Alfred Corney and his crew of the *"Morning Star"* in 1917	195
238	The ketch *"Mouse"* when owned in Cardigan awaiting entry to the port on Teifi Bar.	195
239	The *"Ocean Gem"* at Rolle Quay, Barnstaple in the 1920s. The inside vessel is the *"Bessie Clark"*	196
240	The ketch *"Pleiades"* in Minehead Harbour	198
241	*"Rainbow"* proceeds to sea	199
242	The *"Result"* at Ilfracombe in 1952	201
243	*"Rosetta"* when newly purchased by Stephen Chugg about 1907.	202
244	*"Rosetta"*, proceeding under auxiliary motor	202
245	*Rosetta"* lying at Bude, 8 June 1940	203
246	The auxiliary ketch *"Saint Austell"* at Avonmouth Old Docks.	204
247	The *"Saint Austell"* alongside Appledore Quay at high tide.	205
248	The three crew of the *"Saint Austell,"* complete with three dogs!	205
249	The *"Saint Austell"* aground on the Half Tide Rock at Carlingford Lough, 18 February 1916.	206
250	The ketch *"Saltash"*, previously the *"Iron King"* of Braunton, and before that the *"Desmond"* under which name the entry for this vessel appears.	206
251	The *"Traly"* on her first trip to Bude for her new owners in 1937	210
252	The *"Traly"* entering Bude	210
253	*"Traly"* on the blocks for her annual maintenance.	211
254	*"Traly"* at Rolle Quay, Barnstaple, in 1939	212
255	The ketch *"Trio"* seen at Ilfracombe in 1897	213
256	The ketch *"Two Sisters"*	214
257	The *"Two Sisters"* in the Richmond Dry Dock at Appledore	215
258	*"Woodcock"* at Ilfracombe in 1930 with Captain George Chugg.	218
259	Ketch *"Woodcock"* at Velator in 1936	219
260	*"Woodcock"* discharging at Bude	220
261	The ketch *"Yeo"* at Blue Weir, September 1903	221
262	The crew of the *"Yeo"* pose at the bows for their photograph shortly before she was lost in 1915.	221
	Chart showing entrance to Braunton Pill	Inside rear

From a chart of Barnstaple & Bideford surveyed by Cdr. G. M. Alldridge, Mr. D. Hall, master and W. Quinn, RN, 1855 with small corrections to 1908.

INTRODUCTION

The concept for this work started when the remains of 'Blinking Billy' were discovered around seven years ago and set Robert D'Arcy Andrew on a quest of research. Over many years and as one of the prime movers of Braunton Museum he has collected a huge amount of information pertaining particularly to Braunton's maritime past.

With a group of co-authors apart from Robert, principally Peter Thomson, Tom Welch and David Clement, and the willing loan of many photographs of the vessels that were once so often to be seen on the narrow waterway leading to Braunton, or more properly to Velator Quay, this record has been produced.

The aim of this book is to list each known vessel, with details of measurement and ownership, that was connected with or owned in Braunton and the immediate hinterland, and to give some idea how this came about and in what trades these vessels participated. It is perhaps surprising that Braunton should find itself to all intents and purposes the last home of the sailing coaster, albeit powered with an auxiliary engine at the time of its final demise.

Peter Thomson has painted an evocative picture of the last trades of these vessels in what was by any stretch of the imagination a hard and uncompromising business, offering scant rewards, apart from the periods of the two World Wars. It is perhaps surprising that in a mainly agrarian community a group of men – and women – had grown up who together owned and operated these small cargo-carrying sailing craft, and at the same time provided the resources to service their needs ashore, by way of sailmakers, riggers and general handymen and – once the ubiquitous marine auxiliary came into fashion - engineers. Braunton seamen were amongst the first to utilise the auxiliary engine which, whilst initially under-powered, soon became the principal means of propulsion with reliance upon the wind becoming less.

The last auxiliary sailing cargo-carrier, and perhaps the most famous, was the steel schooner – albeit a ketch-rigged vessel by the time of her demise - *"Result"*, which the late Basil Greenhill has described as amongst the best in her class. She has been described by Tom Welch who with his father Peter sailed in her before embarking upon a career at sea, and by Robert Andrew who felt the same call of the sea as other local men. North Devon and the towns of Bideford, Appledore and to a lesser extent Barnstaple, were amongst the last places operating cargo carrying sail-powered vessels – long after practically the whole of the United Kingdom had given this up. Primarily it was because of the cargoes of basic slag from South Wales, coal, especially from Lydney, the port of the Forest of Dean, and animal feed carried locally to ports around the Bristol Channel and to Ireland, where cargoes could be landed on local beaches and manhandled into horse and cart until the motor lorry came into fashion, and once the convenience of this mode of transport was fully appreciated, quickly took what trade remained.

The entrance to the con-joined Taw and Torridge estuaries has always been difficult of access with the heavy groundswell that can build up on the bar being a trap for the unwary. Robert has written about the entrance and the development of the marking of a safe passage through the bar over a period of time. The numbers of wrecks on the sands of Braunton and nearby Saunton are legion and David Clement with Robert has provided a not exhaustive list of the principal wrecks in this area over time, and reviewed the provision of Braunton's own lifeboat to assist in saving lives.

Whilst the bar was always regarded as a trap to be treated with caution, it did provide a ready source of sand and gravel taken by local builders merchants up until the late 1960s. The high point of this trade was during the huge dock developments from the middle 1870s in South Wales and the Bristol Channel ports with their insatiable appetite for gravel to manufacture concrete.

David Clement

ACKNOWLEDGMENTS:

On behalf of Braunton Museum, I must firstly thank the Awards For All Big Lottery Fund for making the production of this work possible, as they have generously agreed to meet the cost of printing the book, for which we are truly grateful as it could not have been done without this assistance.

Many people and organisations have assisted in the production of this work principally the North Devon Museum Trust (shortened to 'Appledore Museum' in the text), Braunton Museum, Braunton Parish Council, The Admiralty Hydrographic Office (permission to print an old chart of the entrance to the estuaries); Ilfracombe Museum, and various individuals: Keith Andrew, Charmian Astbury, Ken Atherton and the Hydrographic Office, Len Baglole, Catriona Batty, Richard Bros, Roger Chugg, Bill Cook, the late James Dew, Jean Dixon and Robert Jones (information on Reuben Chappell); Elizabeth Dyer, the late S. E. Ellacott, Peter Ferguson, Pamela Gott, John Hartnoll, the late Peter Herbert, Brian Hernaman, Joan Incledon, Peter Incledon, Stephen Knight, the R. L. Knight Collection, Paul and Jean McDine, James Miller, Bill Mitchell who has given freely of his huge photographic collection; Mark Mitchell, Sam Mitchell, Mark Myers, who owns the collection of the late Michael Bouquet; Peter Newcombe, Rachel Nichols, Charles Potter, Sarah Sankey, Jon Seagrave, Gail Shepherd, Frank and Christine Skinner, Dale Thomas and his late father Hugh, Des Tucker, Eric Voysey, Peter Welch, and Tom Welch. If I have left anyone out I do apologise.

My most grateful thanks must go to Andrew Byrom, without whose many hours of travelling, photographing paintings, sourcing photographs and generally overloading his computer this book would not have been possible, and also to David Clement who undertook the complicated task of putting the whole book together.

To each and every one of you, I thank you for making this possible.

Robert D'Arcy Andrew

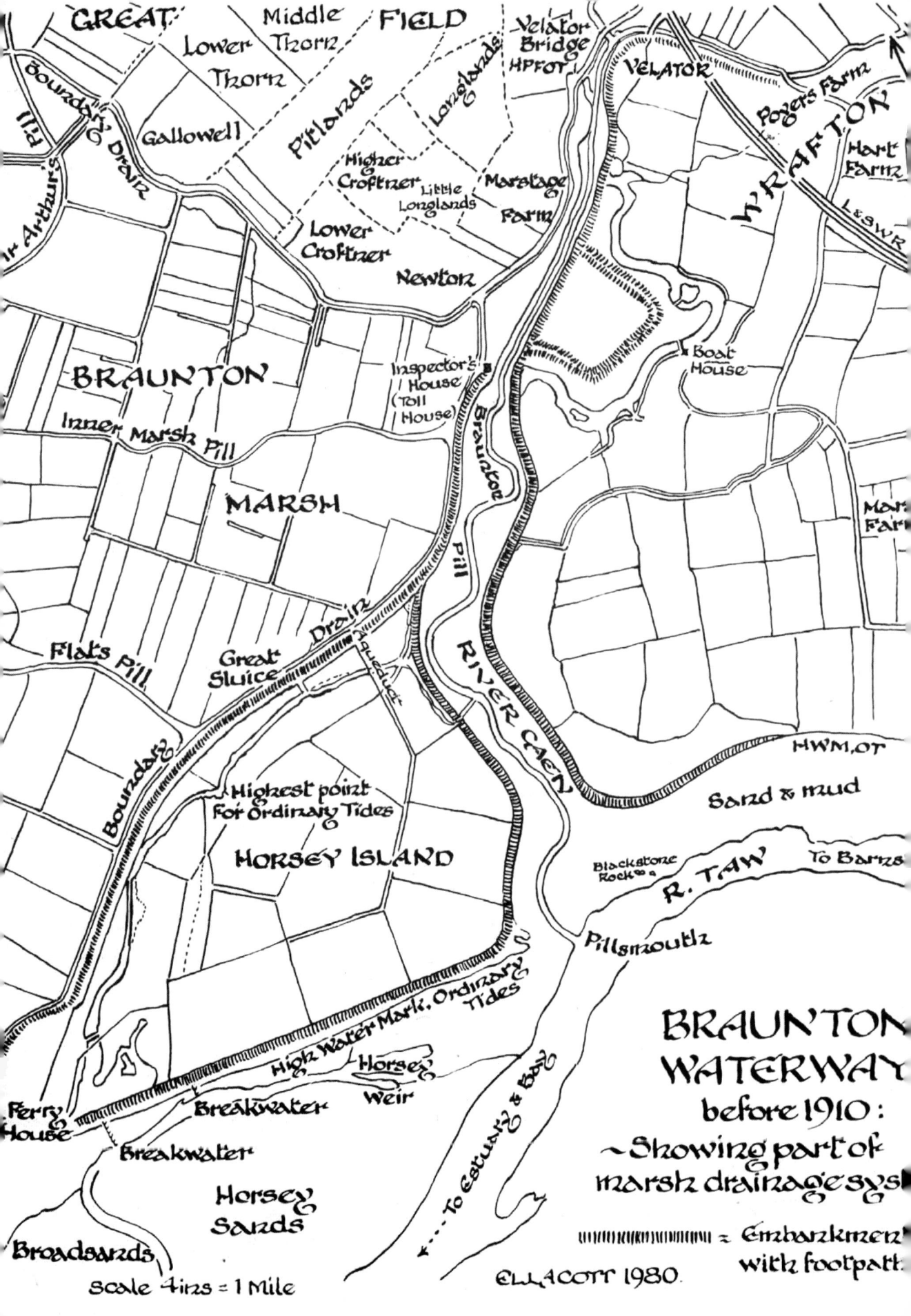

1. BRAUNTON: HOME OF THE LAST FLEET OF SAILING COASTERS

Peter Thomson

By the nineteenth century there was a tradition in the large North Devon village of Braunton of ownership of coastal trading vessels. This arose initially from the need to transport local agricultural produce to market centres. From the 1840's the fleet expanded with the purchase of one or two vessels almost every year. For the next thirty years most, though not all, of those were still small smacks plying locally. Thereafter the size of the vessels increased as they ranged further afield. The fleet continued to grow until the outbreak of the First World War. Between the wars, unlike elsewhere, there was little decline at Braunton; and after the Second World War most of the schooners and ketches that survived in the West Country were owned there. Why Braunton? Indeed why had this village, two miles up a narrow creek (or "pill") off the Taw / Torridge estuary, and with only one small wharf, become such a significant ship-owning centre in the first place?

Braunton Pill is the outlet into the Taw of the River Caen. Originally the Caen had two mouths divided by Horsey Island, a salt marsh. In the eighteenth century ships loaded grain in one or other of those mouths, grain that will have been brought down the Caen from Braunton in small barges. Velator, at the downstream end of Braunton village and at the tidal limit, was above an awkward loop in the river. It was therefore easier for such ships as did come upstream to berth in the loop on the Wrafton side below Velator. In 1811 an embankment was built to enclose the land on the western side of the pill. In the late 1850's this was extended to enclose Horsey Island and reduce the western of the two arms of the lower Caen to a drainage ditch, thereby widening the other arm. In 1860 a suitably embanked cut was then completed which by-passed the loop further upstream and straightened the course of the river.[1] This made Velator considerably more accessible to larger vessels, and justified the building of the present quay there, together with the excavation of a swinging basin.

Throughout this period Braunton men, both "mariners" and merchants, had owned ships.[2] In the 1840's and 1850's, with sometimes controversial national legislation to stimulate trade, they registered a number of brigantines (probably, from their small size, "polaccas), schooners, and, from 1856, ketches. But the greater number of their vessels were still small trading smacks of under 30 tons. These will have been used to bring to Braunton (and elsewhere in North Devon, including open beaches) coal and limestone from South Wales and bricks from Bridgwater, and to take out agricultural produce and

---

[1] See Vols. 9 and 12 of Commander Gammon's manuscript local history notes, held at Braunton Museum.

[2] Although the scale grew substantially in the 19th century, Braunton ship ownership was not new: in the early 17th century four trading vessels are recorded as being owned there - see Michael Oppenheim, A Maritime History of Devon (Exeter 1968, but first prepared in 1908 as a chapter for a projected second Devon volume for the Victoria History of the Counties of England), 59. The Bristol Channel historian Grahame Farr concluded, however, that there was no evidence of shipbuilding at Braunton.

1. The gravel barge "Hilda", with the ketches "Ann" (centre) and "Bessie" (right) at Braunton
Photograph courtesy R. L. Knight

also manganese ore from a nearby mine. What is noticeable from the Barnstaple shipping register of the time is that after Velator was connected more directly to the estuary there were two new features of the pattern of ship-owning: almost all those registering ships were listed as master mariners (rather than just mariners) and already owned at least one other vessel.

But a further and more significant change is to be seen after the opening of the Barnstaple-Ilfracombe railway in 1874. That was a time of agricultural depression, when available rural capital was being drawn to more buoyant sectors of an otherwise expanding economy. As more local distribution shifted to the developing railway network, locally owned ships became larger so that they could lift bigger cargoes covering a wider range of commodities, and thus exploit opportunities further afield. But most remained of a size that could conveniently negotiate Braunton Pill. Thus, although a number of bigger schooners and ketches were registered in that last quarter of the nineteenth century, the typical Braunton-owned trading vessel of the period, with fifteen registrations, was the 35-60 ton ketch. An example was the 45-ton *Bessie Clark*, ordered new for completion in 1881 and owned by the Clarke family in Braunton until she was condemned in 1946 after wartime balloon barrage service. Interestingly, like most of the other vessels in this class at the time, she was wholly owned, with all sixty-four shares, by the master mariner who ordered her. Moreover it is in this period, the 1880's that a number of families emerge as leaders in the field: Drakes, Chuggs, Clarkes, Chichesters, and Watts. These are the names that then appear in the record of the inaugural meeting of the Braunton Shipowners Mutual Marine Assurance Association in 1899. An indication of the regard in which they were held is that within two years of the establishment of the Association, five Appledore vessels were added to the list of ships covered, and that another two years later representatives of two well-known Appledore

2. The ketch "Lewisman" (left) and the "Maude", lying in Braunton Pill – Bill Mitchell.

ship-owning families (Slade and Quance) were members of the committee.[3]

By 1910, probably the heyday of the Braunton fleet when three ships might be discharging at Velator at the same time,[4] the Mutual Assurance Association listed twenty eight vessels owned in or around the village, as well as seventeen from Appledore and four from Ilfracombe. Captain George Welch, who later owned the ketch *Emily Barratt* for thirty years to 1959, remembered in the late 1970's that about a third of that fleet were "down homers", trading only within the Bristol Channel. The three Braunton schooners (*Result*, *William Martyn*, and *Waterlily*) and a few of the biggest ketches worked anywhere within the home trade limits of Ushant to the Elbe, while the rest, medium-sized ketches, traded in the Bristol Channel, Irish Sea, and the western end of the English Channel.[5] For the latter class a facsimile held aboard the restored ketch *Bessie Ellen* of the ship's cargo book for the period reveals the range of typical freights: coal, clay, cement, stone, maize, oats, salt, and manure. It was at this point that the first auxiliary engines were fitted. Braunton owners made this move as early as any coastal trading vessel owners in the country, installing motors in the *Bessie Clark* in 1909 and in the ketch *Edith* in 1910.[6] By 1914 several more ships had been so fitted.

---

[3] Braunton Shipowners Mutual Marine Assurance Association (BSMMAA) minute book 1899-1907, held by Tom Welch. Although by the beginning of the twentieth century the Clarke family always included the 'e' in their name, photographs show that George Clarke's ketch *Bessie Clark* retained the spelling of her 1881 registry entry. The BSMMAA covered half of each ship's declared value - see W.J.Slade and Basil Greenhill, West Country Trading Ketches (London 1974), 24.

[4] Stanley Rogers, Notes on Braunton's Seagoing Trade (republished by the Braunton Museum in 1997)

[5] S.E.Ellacott, Braunton Ships and Seamen (South Molton, Devon, 1980), 57-9. For the "down-homers", the limestone trade between the Gower coast of South Wales and the coasts of Somerset and North Devon had come to an end by 1900 - see W.N.Jenkins, Limestone Quarrying at Pwlldhu, The Gower Society Magazine (1977), 32.

[6] Ellacott, *Braunton Ships and Seamen* (2001 reprint), 70. The *Edith* was sunk in a collision in 1912.

3. The ketch "Bessie" unloading coal at Velator – photo courtesy Braunton Museum

The First World War had a mixed effect on West Country coastal shipping. Memoirs of the period confirm that the extra demands of a war economy on the national transport system kept the vessels busy and freight rates high. Moreover a voyage record for 1917 for the ships covered by the Mutual Assurance Association shows that at least then, when unrestricted U-boat attacks were at their height, the Braunton fleet was largely employed in the Bristol Channel and Irish Sea, with only a handful of vessels (particularly the ketches *St Austell* and *Democrat*) making the more dangerous, though very lucrative, cross-Channel trip to Cherbourg and the Breton ports of St Malo and Morlaix.[7] This will be why the same records only list two Braunton vessels (the schooners *Waterlily* and *William Martyn*) as war losses for that year. But several ships are also listed as laid up during the war, no doubt due to manning difficulties; and because the shipping boom afterwards only lasted for a brief period, most of those seem not to have been brought back into trade.

The economy gradually improved during the 1920's. The Braunton-owned schooners (*Result*, *Four Brothers*, *Morning Star*, (briefly) *Elsie*, and, from 1923, *Eilian*) resumed trading widely within home trade limits.[8] Some of the smaller ketches, particularly the *Bessie*, *Anne*, and *A.T.*, ran regularly to Braunton,[9] while some of the larger ones, such

---

[7] Record of Subscriptions to the BSMMAA 1900-39, held by Tom Welch. The schooner *Result* was an exception. That year she was commissioned as a Q ship, and in that capacity fought two actions against U boats in the North Sea - see Michael Bouquet, No Gallant Ship (London 1959), 182-4. As an indication of how dangerous the English Channel was in 1917, no less than nine sailing vessels of the Fowey-based Stephens fleet alone were sunk there during that year - see Basil Greenhill, *The Merchant Schooners* (London, 4th edition, 1988), 215-6. Much of that traffic was accounted for by a high demand in France for imported coal following the loss of many of the mines in the eastern part of the country.

[8] Both the *Four Brothers* and the *Morning Star* were lost by foundering in 1923. The *Elsie*, at 104ft and 137 tons (net) the biggest vessel owned in Braunton but never successful, was broken up there in 1925.

[9] J.Jenkins ed., *Braunton's Twentieth Century Mariners* (Braunton Museum 2002), 21.Other "down homers"

*4. The steel schooner "Result" (left) and the wooden ketch "Bessie" at Velator in 1939
photo courtesy Braunton Museum*

as the *Emily Barratt* and *Clara May*, sailed as regularly, mainly with coal, to southern Ireland. A good description of life in 1927 aboard a small "down homer" sailing ketch (the 25 ton *Lily*, just sold by a Lynmouth coal merchant to the Weston Clevedon and Portishead Light Railway Company) is contained in Edmund Eglinton's memoir: the delight of sailing close-hauled up the Bristol Channel early on a fresh, bright morning after the back-breaking labour the day before of shovelling out 60 tons of coal in a dried-out harbour; the anxiety of negotiating under sail the "shoots" of the lower River Severn on the way to load another coal cargo at the Forest of Dean terminal of Lydney; and the unreasonable impatience of new owners who had little understanding of the limitations of sailing vessels.[10] To be fair, these were by this time rare. Auxiliary engines (and a reduced rig) had become normal, though the very last Braunton ketch to trade under sail alone, the *Bonita*, was still without one when she was wrecked on the Glamorganshire coast in 1934.[11]

---

had other regular runs: the *Maud* and the *Acacia*, for example, ran regularly between Avonmouth or Barry and Barnstaple or Bideford with flour and grain.

[10] Edmund Eglinton, The Last of the Sailing Coasters (London 1982), 69-84. The *Lily* had actually been fitted with an engine that year, but in Eglinton's time aboard her it never worked.

[11] Barnstaple Shipping Register 1856-1906, NDRO 3318 / S / 3. In April 1933 the *Bonita* entered the estuary, and the next day proceeded to Bideford, under sweeps in the absence of wind - see Greenhill in The Merchant Schooners, 106. The cost of supply and installation of an engine in 1929 to the ketch *Maud*, probably the last of the Braunton-owned vessels to be so fitted, was £195 - see account book for 1918-32 of the P.K. Harris shipyard, held by Michael Guegan of Appledore. This was a significant investment against the rate of return an owner could expect - see next paragraph but one.

5. The ketch "Ann" (left) and the ketch "Bessie" at Velator with Tom Slee, on the bank with a bag and John (Jan 'Bull') Mitchell in the ship's boat.- R. L. Knight Collection

Meanwhile the Braunton fleet gradually grew again to a level close to its pre-1914 size. The peak year between the wars was 1929, when the owners of twenty-five Braunton vessels, and thirteen from Appledore, subscribed to the Association. But that high point was followed by the slump of the early 1930's. The initial reaction to that seems to have been for shipowners to lay up when necessary rather than to sell out, and only in 1933 does a small reduction in the fleet begin to show in the records. But times were nonetheless hard for the majority who kept going. W.J.Slade describes in his autobiography how the economies that had to be made included crew reductions, putting great pressure on masters who at that stage were also expected to act as engineers.[12]

A good picture of this climate is provided by the master's account book of one of the two schooners still owned in Braunton The most regular of the *Result*'s runs was from Newport in South Wales to Torpoint, on the River Tamar opposite Plymouth, with coal. Before the slump the rate was 7 shillings a ton. From 1931 to 1933 that went down to 6s/6d a ton, with the master, from whose two thirds share running costs were paid, ending some trips in deficit. More runs became debits for the master in 1934 when the rate fell first to 5s/9d, then to 5s/3d. At this point he gave up hauling coal from Wales to Cornwall, and switched to carrying cement and stone along the south coast of England. But until 1937 half of those trips ended in deficit too.[13] Nor was the *Result* the only Braunton vessel to leave the Bristol Channel: the 58-ton auxiliary ketch *Mary Eliezer*, which became a regular visitor to Lyme Regis, also earned her living on the south coast

---

[12] W.J.Slade, *Out of Appledore* (London, 4th edition, 1980), 88-9.
[13] *Democrat/Result* Master's Account Book 1920-1937, held by Tom Welch.

*6. The smack "Hilda" unloading gravel at Velator taken from the Bar. The difference in size of the vessels can be clearly seen with the ketch "Bessie" lying behind.
Courtesy Braunton Museum*

at that time, as did the Dutch-built *Crown of Denmark*, which ran between the Isle of Wight and Topsham with cement.[14] Things were a little better for the 34-ton "down homer" ketch *Bessie*, which had a regular run carrying coal from Lydney to Braunton and Barnstaple, and gravel and sand from the estuary to Clevedon, Bristol, and Gloucester. Although the rate for the owner's third of a coal freight to Braunton generally held up at £5-13s, that for coal to Barnstaple went down to £4-17s-6d; while a third share of a gravel cargo fell from £3-10s-0d to £3-0-0.[15] Judging again from this small sample, the economic upturn from 1937 brought little improvement in freight rates. But as the number of vessels active did not continue to fall in the late 1930's, there must at least have been more work for them. There was also once again the prospect of war and the better rates that was likely to offer.

Gordon Mote, a schoolboy at the time, describes a typical week aboard a Braunton-owned auxiliary "down homer", the 30-ton *Enid*, in the summer of 1939, just before the start of events that were to lead to the decimation of the fleet. As so often, the *Enid* undertook a four-legged voyage: to Neath (between Swansea and Port Talbot) with sand loaded at the Taw/Torridge estuary mouth; from there light to Penarth (on the Welsh coast east of Swansea); from Penarth to Lynmouth (on the north Devon coast east of Ilfracombe) with coal; and back to Braunton for the weekend. With a fair wind in each case, and only a 30 horsepower engine, the first and third legs were under sail. But, in order to avoid the need for ballast, the second was under motor, as were entering and leaving harbour. It is striking that between Neath and Penarth alone they passed three

---

[14] Basil Greenhill, The Ketch Mary Eliezer - a Link with the Riddle of the Sands (September 2001 draft article for a Yorkshire periodical) and Ellacott in Braunton Ships and Seamen (2001 reprint), 39.

[15] *Bessie* Cargo Book 1911-1943, held by Tom Welch. These rates of return should be compared with examples of costs of repairs to Braunton ketches that owners had to bear in 1931: £165 for general repairs (probably to meet Board of Trade certificate reqirements) to the *Mary Stewart* and £166 for similar work on the *Dido C,* not to speak of £268 for a new keel for the *St Austell* in 1929 and £329 for sheathing of the *Bessie Clark* in 1928 - see P.K.Harris account book 1918-32

*7. The ketches (left to right) "Acacia", "Lizza", "Murray" and "Bonita" in Appledore Pool
Photograph courtesy Appledore Museum*

schooners and five ketches from the Bar ports (Barnstaple, Bideford, Appledore, and Braunton) on their way elsewhere.[16] But as a sign of the difficulty of earning a reasonable living in auxiliary coasters in the 1930's, if perhaps also because of the accommodation space given up to the engine, their regular third hand of earlier days was no longer shipped. This in turn will have been one reason why the *Enid* was by that time rigged, unusually, with a Bermudan (or "leg of mutton") mainsail as well as, more normal for auxiliaries, mizzen. These will have been lighter to work than the gaff sails traditionally associated with West Country trading vessels; and the likely reduction in the drive produced will have been acceptable with an end to windward sailing.[17]

With the outbreak of war at the end of that summer, freight rates for coasters rose substantially almost at once, as the new need to move munitions began to over-burden the railways. This is confirmed in memoirs, and borne out by the *Bessie*'s cargo book: the rate for a coal cargo went up by 30% in late 1939 and by another 20% on the original figure the following year, while that for gravel increased by a third. By 1943 the rate for

---

[16] Gordon Mote, *The West Countrymen* (Bideford 1986), 9-11.
[17] Slade in *Out of Appledore*, 91-3, tells, on the other hand, how he changed the leg of mutton mainsail he had rigged on his schooner *Haldon* back to a gaff sail because of the undue strain exercised by the peak of the former on the masthead. A 1947 photograph indicates that by then the *Enid* too had reverted to a gaff mainsail.

8. The "C.F.H." lying at Velator – Peter Welch

coal was more than double the pre-war level. Although some trade to Ireland continued, most of the vessels not commandeered by the government were kept busy in the Bristol Channel. The two schooners, *Result* and *Eilian*, made regular coal runs to, respectively, Highbridge (at the mouth of the Bridgwater river) and Ilfracombe, plus occasional trips up Braunton Pill with gravel for the extension of the former civil airfield at Chivenor; whilst among the ketches the *Crown of Denmark*, for example, returned from the English Channel to haul scrap metal from Bristol to Llanelli, and the *Garlandstone*, a little later, moved from the Irish trade to a regular run from the Welsh ports to Watchet in Somerset.[18] For those trading to Ilfracombe, as well as Lynmouth and the small ports of west Somerset, there was a boom in demand for return cargoes of pit props from the Exmoor valleys for the Welsh coal mines.[19] This combination of better freight rates, more return shipments, and, overall, more intense activity meant that there was at last money to be made out of these obsolete ships.

In places other than the Taw/Torridge estuary, West Country owners nonetheless continued to get rid of their sailing and auxiliary sailing vessels. Following the dispersal of the remains of the unpowered Stephens fleet from Fowey in 1938 and 1939,[20] and then the unrigging early in the war of the other three schooners still owned in south Cornwall,[21] the last-but-one Bridgwater ketch was sold away in 1943 and last two Gloucester-owned schooners in 1946.[22] Although single vessels were still owned after

---

[18] *Result* Cargo Book 1929-52, held by Tom Welch; Daily Telegraph 5 September 1957 (when the *Eilian*'s sale was announced - she was reported to have been "almost exclusively engaged" in carrying coal from Lydney to Ilfracombe since 1941); Ellacott, *Braunton Ships and Seamen* (2001 reprint), 39; and Jenkins ed., 21 and 14.

[19] Grahame Farr, *Ships and Harbours of Exmoor* (Williton, Somerset), 39.

[20] John Anderson, *Coastwise Sail,* (London 1948), 37 and 64.

[21] ibid., 45, 50, and 57. The vessels were the *Katie, Mary Miller*, and *SF Pearce*.

[22] James Nurse, *The Nurse Family of Bridgwater and their Ships* (London 1999), 25 and Norah Ayland, *Schooner Captain* (Truro 1972), 147. The ships were the ketch *Sunshine* and the schooners *Camborne* and *Ryelands*.

9. The ketch "Enid" lying at Velator Quay – courtesy Bill Mitchell

the war in Bridgwater, Minehead, and Bude,[23] it was only from Braunton and Appledore that any number of these ships remained active. Of those, the majority were owned in Braunton.

In 1939 there had been nine schooners and twenty-four ketches from the estuary still trading.[24] All were auxiliaries.[25] Between then and late 1944, when there were no losses to enemy action, four Braunton ketches were sold away (*A.T., Dido C., Two Sisters*) or wrecked (*Woodcock*). But of that great majority of Braunton and Appledore vessels that remained on the Mutual Assurance Association's books,[26] ten, over a third, had been requisitioned early in the war for balloon barrage service; and all but three of those were condemned with the return of peace in 1945.[27] 1946 and 1947 then saw a further cull: five Braunton ketches (as well as one of two remaining Appledore schooners

---

[23] The auxiliary ketches *Irene* (sold out of trade in 1960) at Bridgwater, *Emma Louise* (laid up in 1953) at Minehead, and *Traly* (sold to Danish owners in 1958) at Bude.

[24] These figures are taken from BSMMAA records. Greenhill in *The Merchant Schooners*, 263, puts the number of ketches at thirty-two.

[25] The only engine-less coastal trading vessels in the West Country in 1939 were the schooners *Katie* and *Mary Miller*, both owned in Par and laid up during the Second World War.

[26] see letter Clarke/Jerram 6 November 1944, reproduced in Vol.3 of H.Oliver Hill's manuscript notebook on coastal craft, held at the National Maritime Museum, Greenwich.

[27] The only three vessels returned to trade from balloon barrage service were the Braunton-owned ketches *Democrat* and *Emily Barratt* and the Appledore-owned ketch *Progress*. Vessels condemned then included the Appledore schooners *Earl Cairns, Margaret Hobley, Donald and Doris, M.A.James,* and *Welcome*. The record of only two losses to weather throughout the Second World War (the ketches *Woodcock* in 1943 and *Minnie Flossie* in 1945), against four for 1917 alone a quarter of a century before, shows how much the fitting of auxiliary engines had improved ship safety.

10. The "Acacia" (foreground) and the "Crown of Denmark" at Big Quay.

and one of three remaining Appledore ketches) were sold[28] or hulked, as resources were concentrated on refits for those hulls in the best shape.

What this post-war adjustment left for Braunton owners was the two steel schooners that had belonged to them in 1939 (*Result* and *Eilian*, neither of which had been requisitioned) and nine ketches, all but two of wooden construction. Because of an acute general shortage of shipping following war losses, there was a place for them in the coastal trade. But the wartime drive for efficiency had imparted to shippers higher expectations for delivery, and there was less patience with traditional loading and discharge methods among port operators.[29] This led owners of ships built as sailing vessels to widen hatches and fit steel coamings, to reduce windage by shortening pole masts and bowsprits, and, above all, to fit more powerful - if almost always second hand[30] - engines and winches. This turned the surviving schooners and ketches, at least for most of the time, from auxiliary sailing vessels into motor vessels with steadying sails.

Peter Herbert describes a voyage in the period immediately following this final effort to maintain the viability of such former sailing coasters as were left. At the end of 1950, the

---

[28] Three (*Bessie Ellen*, *Mary Eliezer*, and *Crown of Denmark*) of the four that were sold went to Denmark. The fourth (*Bessie*) was sold out of trade. The vessel hulked was the *Maud*. The Appledore-owned vessels that remained after 1947 were the ketches *St Austell* (sold out of trade in 1951 and lost the following year) and *Progress* (withdrawn from trade in 1952 after hull straining, sold in 1954, and soon abandoned); and the schooner *Kathleen and May* (sold out of the Irish trade in 1960 and preserved by successive owners, most recently a Bideford businessman, Steve Clarke). The number of Barnstaple-owned vessels, which in the nineteenth century exceeded the figure for Braunton by a considerable margin, dwindled between the wars. None remained in trade after the ketch *Lewisman* was laid up in 1946 and sold to Scottish owners soon afterwards.

[29] These attitudes are well described in Richard England, *Schoonerman* (London 1981).

[30] Letter from the late Peter Herbert, former master of the ketch *Agnes*, 25 August 2002.

11. "Maud Mary" (left), the ketch "Thomas" and the "Trio (right) off Appledore – courtesy Appledore Museum

76-ton Appledore ketch *Progress* loaded a cargo of scrap-iron at Southampton for Port Talbot in Wales. As was to be expected at that time of year, she had to make her way down-Channel against strong headwinds. Interestingly this called, with a 70 horsepower engine, for motor-sailing under standing jib and reefed mainsail, first on one tack, then on the other, rather than bashing straight into the weather under engine alone. But what is also striking to the modern reader is that during that leg of the trip the crew of three, two of whom were elderly men, had to man the pumps constantly and then, as the wind increased to gale force and as they became exhausted, to take shelter in Falmouth.[31] Those working conditions and those operating limits were not going to be acceptable for long in the post-war world. Being able to sail without the motor with the wind aft, as the *Progress* did once "round the land" and in the Bristol Channel, would not be an adequate compensation.

These pressures made themselves felt only slowly during the 1950's. But the result of their impact, and of the slowly increasing availability of more modern shipping and better road haulage, was a further erosion of the competitiveness of the former sailing coasters, now almost entirely in the hands of Braunton owners. Distribution of coal in particular, the coasters traditional mainstay, was shifting to the roads, except in the cases of more isolated places where there were gasworks, such as Ilfracombe, where the schooner *Eilian* retained a supply contract, and Minehead, where the ketch *Mary Stewart* took over delivery from a local vessel in 1953.[32] For the rest, the *Result* moved back in 1952 to the English Channel, where she hauled bagged lime from Plymouth and Brixham to the Channel Islands, phosphate from Granville (in Normandy) to Jersey, and granite chippings from Guernsey to the Thames; the ketch *Emily Barratt* carried the odd cargo of

---

[31] Peter Herbert, *Home for Christmas,* Ships Monthly, December 1994.
[32] Farr in *Ships and Harbours of Exmoor*, 24 and 43. The *Mary Stewart* replaced the auxiliary ketch *Emma Louise* after a survey showed that work on the latter needed for recertification would cost £1000.

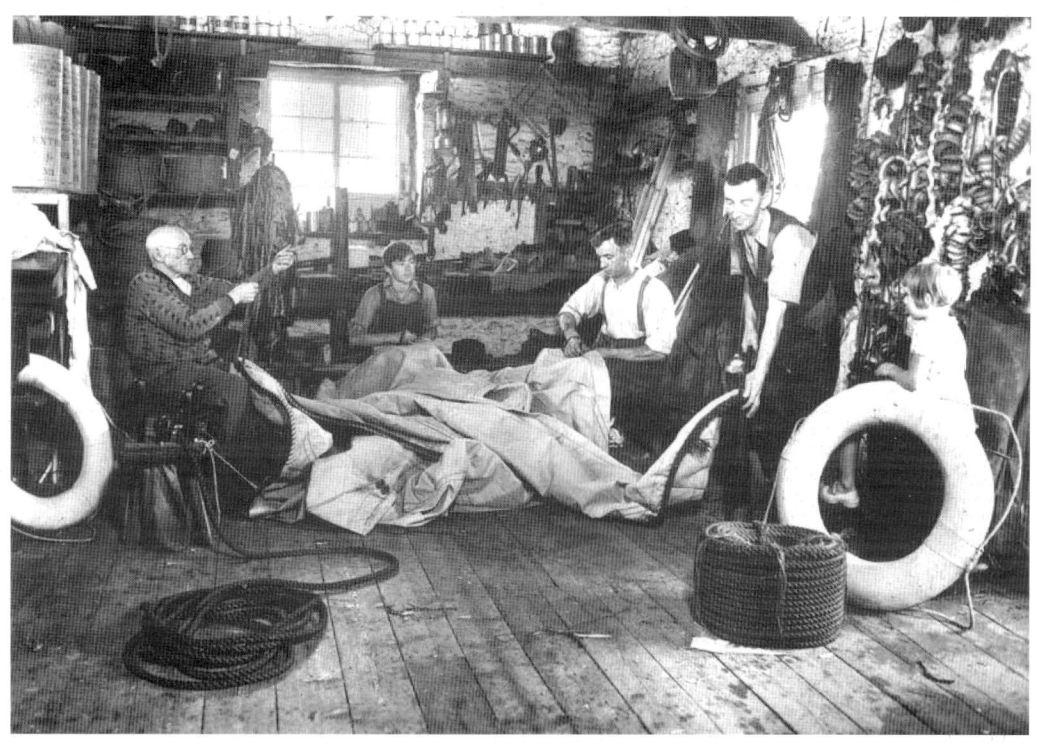

12. Braunds, the local sailmakers

building materials from Bridgwater to Ireland; and the other ketches found themselves almost exclusively engaged in the Bristol Channel trade in grain, flour, and animal feed between Barnstaple, Bideford, Avonmouth, Gloucester and the Welsh ports.[33] There were also occasional coal trips "around the land" to the Scilllies and Penzance, and periods in the early 1950's when slag (for fertiliser) was carried from Swansea to Barnstaple and Bideford.[34] Braunton itself, in the shape of Velator quay, was little used after the 1940's: the *Result*'s last visit there was in 1948;[35] when preparing his book *Devon Harbours* in 1950, Vernon Boyle found only one ketch in the Pill awaiting news of a charter, and little sign of activity at the quay;[36] and indeed a contemporary item in Tom

---

[33] *Result* Cargo Books 1929-52 and 1953-66; and local press cuttings dated 24 March 1954, held by Tom Welch, and 27 September1957, held by the North Devon Maritime Museum (hereafter NDMM) as MP 6.10.1. As early as 1950 there had been complaints at a BSMMAA meeting that other types of craft were getting preferential treatment in the Bristol Channel grain trade - see BSMMAA minute book 1946-59, NDRO B 120 add 2. Former master of the *Agnes* Bill Mitchell confirmed in conversation in November 2005 that, apart from the *Mary Stewart*'s Minehead coal contract from 1953 to 1958, there was very little work for the ketches in the Bristol Channel in the 1950's other than grain-related freights; and that they were almost all by then working only two-handed.

[34] Local press cuttings dated 30 August 1955, NDMM MP 4.11.4, and 30 May 1958, NDMM MP 6.23.2, reporting the *Eilian* and the Bude-owned *Traly* as having delivered coal to Penzance; local press cutting dated 20 October 1952, NDMM MP2.13.3, reporting the *Democrat* unloading slag at Barnstaple; and conversations in July 2003 with former crew member Robert Andrew on the *Enid*'s involvement in this trade, and in November 2005 with Bill Mitchell on the *Clara May*'s involvement, before the vessels' disposal in 1951 and 1952.

[35] Conversation with Tom Welch, son of her last owner in trade, June 2003.

[36] V.C.Boyle and D.Payne, *Devon Harbours* (London 1952), 181-3. Other small harbours fell out of use in the same period: the ketch *Traly* was the last to unload at Bude in 1946 (see Peter Thomson, *Bude: a Haven not without Risk,* Mariners Mirror 3/87, August 2001), and the *Democrat* at Porlock in 1950 (see

*13. The "St. Austell" (left) and "Maud" of Bideford at Braunton Quay 13 September 1946.
Courtesy Appledore Museum*

Welch's collection of local press cuttings reported that a coal cargo unloaded by the *Mary Stewart* in 1953 was the first for some years.

Although the two schooners still survived, the number of ketches continued to dwindle in the first half of that decade, with further sales out of trade (*Enid* in 1951 and *Democrat* in 1954) and hulkings (*Clara May* and *CFH*, both around 1952) following the loss at sea of the *Hanna* in 1949. 1956 saw the last time when as many as five former sailing coasters were in harbour together, with the Braunton ketches *Agnes*, *Emily Barratt*, and *Garlandstone*, the Bridgwater ketch *Irene*, and the Appledore schooner *Kathleen and May* alongside at Appledore for the Easter holiday.[37] The next three years then saw the end of the Braunton fleet as such. The remaining ketches (*Agnes*, *Garlandstone*, *Mary Stewart*, and *Emily Barratt*) were sold, successively, out of trade, and the schooner *Eilian* to a Danish operator, between 1957 and 1959. The Braunton Shipowners Mutual Marine Assurance Association, which had been only been able to continue after 1947 thanks to provision of extra cover through the wider coastal vessels' club, was wound

---

Grahame Farr, *Somerset Harbours* (London 1954), 159). The trade to open beaches had largely died in the 1930's: a number of visits by the ketch *Agnes* to Watermouth, between Ilfracombe and Lynmouth, in 1942 were probably the very last of their kind (see Jenkins ed., 23).

[37] Local press cutting dated 6 April 1956, NDMM MP 5.3.1.

14. Velator Quay, with from left to right, the "Result" as a 3-masted schooner, ketch "Democrat", the sailing gravel barge "Hilda" and the ex-sailing barge "Rowena" with the hull of the schooner "Elsie" behind, being broken up. – courtesy Braunton Museum

up.[38] The schooner *Result* alone of the Braunton vessels remained in trade. She had been rigged from 1953 with only a foremast and mizzen, though setting a big mizzen staysail instead of the main; and from 1957 with only half a bowsprit.[39] Those modifications made cargo handling and berthing easier. As important, they enabled her owner-skipper to reduce his crew to, besides himself, two men from three;[40] and thus to keep her trading until 1967, when he died.

Why did Braunton shipowners continue to work auxiliary-engined sailing vessels when other seafaring communities were giving them up? Before the Second World War, when times were hard for everyone, they found that there was just enough trade in the Bristol Channel for most of them to make a living. They were helped in that respect by the fact that there was still some demand for the gravel and sand that they could load as outward cargo at low water at next to no cost from deposits just inside the estuary. They had the further advantages over shipowners elsewhere that, with the advent of auxiliary engines, they could lay up their ships between charters inside the Pill free of the charges levied at any fully administered commercial harbour or shipping channel; and that at Velator there was a sailmaker (from 1900), an engine shop (from around 1914), and, until the late 1930's, a timber grid for ships to be laid upon for bottom work by two shipwrights, all of which gave them a degree of independence from shipyards.[41] After the Second World War, during which they had done well, they found themselves with a sizeable fleet of vessels with a very small resale value. The aim therefore became to continue to run those ships that could meet Board of Trade survey requirements without undue expense, for so long as they could make a profit; and they were successful in that for another

---

[38] Records of 1958 and 1959 meetings in BSMMAA minute book 1946-59, NDRO B 120 add. 2.

[39] Local press cuttings dated 30 September 1953, held by Tom Welch, and 21 June 1957, held by the NDMM as MP 5.28.1.

[40] Michael Bouquet, West Country Sail (Newton Abbott 1971), 104.

[41] B.J.Chugg, Captains Clarke of Braunton, Maritime South West No. 16 (2003), 52-3, and Jenkins ed., 16.

fifteen years, broadly the time it took to modernise Britain's transport infrastructure after the war.

There were a number of other factors at work in the sudden demise of the surviving fleet of West Country former sailing coasters as that period drew to an end. The growing demand for quicker delivery undoubtedly took its toll: freights simply became more difficult for owners to come by. So too did the age of the vessels that remained. Four of the five ships disposed of in the late 1950's were built (or, in the case of the *Agnes*, rebuilt) in the twentieth century. But the youngest of them, the *Emily Barratt*, was forty five years old. The predicament of the owners was also aggravated by the prospect of the closure of the Lydney coal terminal (which finally happened in 1960), with which the Barmen had always had a strong connection. But what finished these vessels off was probably as much something else: the collapse of the wherewithal to keep them going as, at sea, elderly skippers and mates called it a day in the absence of younger men to replace them, and as, ashore, shipwrights, sailmakers, and chandlers experienced in the needs of wooden sailing vessels retired or switched to more lucrative work. Press cuttings of the period show that there was a good deal of public interest in the handful of schooners and ketches that struggled on after the war. But that was not enough, in the end, to keep them going beyond their time.

Of those last vessels to trade, only three remain in this country. The *Result* and the *Garlandstone* survive as static exhibits, the former ashore in Ulster, the latter afloat on the River Tamar in the West Country. The *Bessie Ellen*, one of the ketches sold to Denmark in 1947, was brought back to Britain in 2001 by her new owner, Nikki Alford, for restoration as a passenger charter vessel at Plymouth. By a nice coincidence that is where she was built in 1907 for Captain John Chichester of Braunton, whose family continued to own and operate her after his death in 1920 until her sale overseas.

The rise and fall of the fleet in which these three ships worked was thus impelled, as with all commercial enterprise, by economic circumstances. Trade liberalisation probably caused the initial expansion. Development of overland transport infrastructure then changed the pattern of the coastal trade, as did agricultural depression. That called for larger vessels. The First World War disrupted the trade, but enabled money to be made for some subsequent investment in the fleet. Braunton was then better able than elsewhere to weather the slump of the 1930's, because the estuary itself offered an extra opportunity for freight and the "pill" for self-maintenance. Finally there remained, for just over a decade after the Second World War, a place at the margin of the coastal trade for a small number of auxiliary sailing ships, as the economy struggled to get back on its feet and to catch up with the times. By the late 1950's that interval was over.

SOURCES

Except where cross-referenced in the text and the notes, information on ship ownership in the nineteenth century is drawn from the Barnstaple Shipping Registers for 1837-55 and 1856-1906, held at the North Devon Record Office (NDRO) at Barnstaple under accession numbers 3318/S/2 and 3; data on ship numbers from 1900 to 1939 from the Braunton Shipowners Mutual Marine Assurance Association (BSMMAA) subscription records for that period, held by Mr Tom Welch at Ashford, near Braunton; and details of ship disposals from 1920 onwards from the Grahame Farr card index of West Country shipping, held at the National Maritime Museum at Greenwich.

The writer is also grateful to the late Dr Basil Greenhill for suggesting the topic; to Bill Mitchell of Braunton, to Robert Andrew, formerly of Braunton, and to the staff of the museums at Braunton and at Appledore for their advice.

ACKNOWLEDGEMENT: The above was originally published in 2004 as an article in the "*Mariners Mirror*", the journal of the Society for Nautical Research. It is reproduced with the kind permission of the Honorary Editor.

2. LIFE AND TIMES

ROBERT D'ARCY ANDREW

I was born in Braunton in May 1928, then a very different place to what is now part of the extended suburbia of North Devon and the principal town – Barnstaple. Then it was principally an agrarian community, with as an important sideline, the life and neighbourhood associated with the coastal trades of the area through its close connection with the waterways leading to the Taw and Torridge estuaries.

My grandfather owned a 250-acre mixed farm at Boode, Braunton and from an early age I grew up in an agricultural environment – looking across the bay towards Lundy Island, Bideford Bar and Hartland Point. We used to hear the Bull Point foghorn on a regular basis, which carried straight across to us. My father jointly owned the farm with my grandfather and used to specialise in sheep and cattle farming. My father left the farm in 1935 and took us to live at Saunton, where my parents occupied a small boarding house overlooking the beach, not far from the site of the present day Saunton Sands Hotel. The Christie family – who owned most of Saunton - built this in 1935 and it is now operated by the Brend family. It was built by a contractor from Lewes, Sussex, near where the Christie family owned a large estate - Glyndebourne. We were now living directly overlooking the beach at Saunton, my father travelling to the farm daily on an old motorcycle. This continued until grandfather sold the farm in 1938.

When I was about 14, I went into Braunton to try to acquire a seine net to catch fish off the beach at Saunton, and was directed to the local pilot, Jan Crick at Velator who might be persuaded to make one up, having a lot of old nets as he was also a salmon fisherman. He was very easily persuaded and he and I got on wonderfully well. One morning when visiting with him he said that he had to take a boat down from Velator Quay to a mooring at Pill's Mouth, and if I wished I could come with him. Needless to say I did not need asking a second time. I was there! It was approaching Autumn in 1943 when I went on my first trip to "sea" aboard the 60-ton ketch *"Bessie"*, where the master was "Curly" Collins. He always had a cigarette in his mouth, rolling this from one side of his mouth to the other! I can remember this as if it were yesterday. When we left there were no crewmembers – just Curly Collins, Jan Crick and myself. We took in all the mooring ropes and off we went under motor – an old Invincible engine. The Pill was very windy and Jan, who had been an old Navy man and a full time salmon fisherman, was giving the instructions and telling Curly where to steer, "Port a bit" or "Starboard a titch". When we arrived at the mouth, we picked up a mooring buoy and secured, then we rowed ashore and left the ship's boat on the bank and walked back to Velator, and I went back to Saunton on my bicycle. We remained in Saunton until 1944. Our home was leasehold and although my dad had the opportunity to purchase this he refused on principle to buy anything he could not own outright. Over Christmas 1944 we moved to a new home in Braunton on East Hill which was convenient for my father who was now working with an electrical contractor – Chichesters of Braunton.

I was now living in a location adjacent to a number of retired sailing shipmasters and indeed our next door neighbour was Captain Harry Clarke with Captain "Jonto" Clarke nearby, and Captain Steve Chugg immediately adjacent on the other side. This was very much a "waterfront" area, and when I was 16 or 17 I built my first boat in Captain Steve

15. Robert's boat "Salar" ready for launching in 1945, with friends and family celebrating the occasion – Robert Andrew

16. The "Salar", unrigged, at Velator showing the quayside opposite off which lies the small seaweed barge.
Photo by James Miller

17. "Salar" at sea with Captain Steve Chugg enjoying a trip on Robert's boat.
Photo by James Miller

18. The young boatbuilder, aged 17 with Pamela Fowler – the girl next door – and her brother Leonard, aboard the "Salar" at the Bar buoy at dead low water.
Photo by James Miller

Chugg's nearby orchard. It was called "Salar" named after the book *"Salar the Salmon"* by Henry Williamson, and was a 14-foot wood clinker dinghy. Subsequently I went on to build a 20-foot "Yachting Monthly" 3-tonner in a large garage down the road. At this time there were still several sailing vessels based at Braunton. With this maritime influence running through my veins, although I had taken a post as a pupil to the local Barnstaple Rural District Council surveyor and public health inspector, for a period of four years, on every holiday I could get I went off to sea.

The first trip was to Swansea on the 60-ton ketch *Enid* – the smallest coasting vessel owned in Braunton. It was 1945 and the war had just come to an end. We left Velator Quay with no ballast or cargo and sailed over the Bar, which was a bit "bumpy", to Swansea, where we arrived on the afternoon of the same day and entered the North Dock, which no longer exists. This was a regular place for small sailing vessels to congregate adjacent to Weaver's Mill buildings – all now sadly demolished and with the old North Dock filled in. We had motored across the Bristol Channel with some sail set to assist. We loaded some 63 tons of basic slag. Loading was extremely slow, lasting two or three days as there was a strike at the steelworks and lorries would only bring the material intermittently, unloading this onto the quayside and leaving the dockers to load the 1-cwt. bags into the hold of the *"Enid"* via a chute into the vessel's hold.

19. *The ketch "Enid" at Velator, 1947 – Robert Andrew*

There was sufficient time for us to "see the sights" and I remember going to see "Arsenic and Old Lace" at the Swansea theatre on that occasion. Swansea had been terribly blitzed and ruined buildings were all around us. We continued loading until she had reached her capacity, the pile of bags forming only a small mound in the bottom of the hold, as slag is a very heavy cargo, and in no way filled the capacity of the hold. The cargo was consigned to Fulfords of Bideford and was ultimately used for spreading on agricultural land to break up the clay soils. Leaving Swansea in the morning we had arrived at Bideford Bar on the afternoon tide and were secured and ready to discharge by that evening. The crew consisted of the skipper Roland Chichester, who lived at Georgeham, and Reggie Williams the A.B., who was also a very fine cook, and myself as "Third Hand". I don't think I was much help on that occasion, but then they did not seem to need much help – at least from me. My function as I recall was tidying up the paintwork! Discharging took place the following day using a quayside crane.

20. "Result" drying her sails at Ilfracombe, about 1951 – Robert Andrew

In 1946 I received a month's notice for enlistment for National Service, and advised my employer that I wanted a month's holiday, which was granted. I quickly made arrangements to join the *"Result"* at Fremington Quay where she had brought a cargo of coal from Newport. She was busy running steam coal from South Wales to Fremington Quay for the railways, calling at various South Wales ports from Newport to Cardiff. I did three trips on her straight off, taking three of my four weeks, to Newport, twice, and Cardiff on my last trip on that occasion, before being called up on the 26th. September 1946. I remember that whilst in Newport the steamship just ahead of us was discharging a cargo of oranges. The Dockers were very rough in handling the wood crates of oranges and several "came adrift" with oranges all over the quayside. Needless to say a significant quantity found themselves aboard *"Result"* and we had our "five-a-day" for a while! Another "Liberty" ship discharging iron ore at the same time I remember had a Captain "Buffy" Elliott from Church Street, Braunton, whose father was the local blacksmith. Whilst in Cardiff a tremendous equinoctial gale blew up. We were lying in Roath Dock and the wind was so strong that our ropes parted and it was a mad rush to replace these. We strengthened the moorings using wire ropes and no harm befell.

All these trips were under Captain Tom Welch who was a great man for carrying sail. When we left Fremington Quay it was the practice to have all the fore and aft sails set by the time we were in Appledore Pool, and to have the topsails set before we sailed over the Bar. Our passage to the South Wales ports would be mainly under sail with the Widdup 4-cylinder 120-h.p motor running at half power. This motor had been installed the previous January at the same time as the wheelhouse was built fronting the old whaleback shelter. *"Result"* then had a permanent crew of four – the master, Tom Welch, the Mate, Peter Welch, and the A.B., Sam Mitchell and the boy/cook, Tommy Christie. I was taken on as a supernumerary – very much a passenger but one who pulled his weight with the rest. Captain Tom Welch organised the food supplies, and also took charge of cutting the bread! – one slice each. Tommy was not a bad cook having been influenced by the remainder of the crew! On entering port Sam Mitchell would normally take the wheel with Captain Tom Welch by his elbow and Peter Welch up forward to warn of specific obstructions, and with Tommy Christie running around helping wherever needed. Entering the South Wales ports would be carried out under motor only and when leaving, the sails would not be set until the vessel had left the dock. Loading was carried out by dockside gantries which created terrible dust, indeed the vessel and crew were totally coated with black dust by the time loading was complete and the first thing to do was to clean ship and yourselves before leaving. Unloading at Fremington Quay was by grab crane that created nothing like as much dust. We found nothing much to do in Newport but walked into Cardiff and Butetown whilst lying at Roath. After crossing the Bideford Bar, off Appledore we would turn to stem the tide, put the ship's boat over and row to Kilstone Point, opposite Crow Point, where we would pick up the pilot. The master would telephone before leaving advising him of our approximate time of arrival when the pilot – usually one of the Stribling family – would take the vessel up to Fremington.

Having enlisted in the Army I had done my basic training and, coincidentally, afterwards been posted to Fremington Camp, at that time still used for training in amphibious operations. I was in the medical corps and with a "living out" pass sleeping at home in Braunton, being required to inspect locations within a 40-mile radius at various small army camps and prisoner-of-war camps, and to report back to the Medical Officer at Fremington. This allowed me plenty of time to indulge myself in the love of merchant sail and on most weekends and periods of leave I could be found amongst the sailing community.

In August 1947, I was given 10-days leave. I caught Campbell's paddle-steamer from Ilfracombe to Swansea and a bus from there to Port Talbot and joined the *"Result"* which was lying ready-loaded with coal and bound to Gweek, on the Helford River, in Cornwall. Tom Welch was still the skipper with the same crew. Peter's brother, who was in the Royal Navy, Johnny Welch, had been aboard for a short trip previously but was leaving and it was intended I would take his place as "spare hand". After obtaining a drum of lubricating oil that Captain Tom was waiting for we sailed. I well remember that Captain Tom physically tasted the lubricating oil before he would accept this, as he did not totally trust the suppliers. Even had it been Shell he would not trust them! The 40-gallons of oil was decanted into the tank below decks and clearly, once this had been done it was too late to change the material.

When all was ready we sailed on the evening tide for Helford where we arrived a couple of days later. You could only get to Gweek Quay on the top of a spring tide. There was a grab crane on the quayside to assist in discharging, which took a few days, and by the time we had completed unloading, the tides had reduced and the *"Result"* was beneaped, and obliged to wait for a few days until the tide made sufficiently to enable her to leave the berth. In the meantime we tended to live off the land and we went ashore over the fields shooting anything we could find, until the local gamekeeper advised us that "Enough was enough!" I remember we shot a curlew on one occasion, which we skinned and put into a stew with a piece of salt beef, two pounds of tomatoes, and anything edible that would go in – possibly lentils etc – to make what was a tasty stew. Next day we decided we would go over the side and see what we could find at low water by way of flat fish. All five aboard went and we found at least 40-odd flatfish, known locally as "flukes", which we strung together on a piece of wire we had found and carried back our trophies. These were extremely tasty fried with bread. By this time the tide had made sufficiently to turn the vessel at the quayside, and on the top of the tide I remember taking the ship's boat and sculling this to the opposite bank with a long grass rope, which I secured to a holly tree. We hauled the *"Result"* around to face seawards, before leaving on that same tide for Porthoustock to load a cargo of stone chippings for Bristol. We went alongside this huge concrete bin. It took less than 50 minutes to load 163 tons stone chippings sent down the chute at the quarry, following which we sailed, anchoring off Porth Navas. That evening I sculled the skipper ashore to telephone the ship's broker to confirm we were loaded and would be leaving next morning, and to give an estimated time of arrival at Kings Road, outside the Avon. When we arrived we were able to sail directly up the river Avon to the Cumberland Basin, which we entered on the same tide. As we went under the Clifton suspension bridge I remember some boys throwing pebbles down on our vessel. We tied up on the right hand side of the basin just above the current location of the ss. *"Great Britain"* on the town council's quay. It was Saturday evening and I was due back to Fremington Camp the following day – so had to move fairly smartish. We found a paddle steamer sailing the next day and on the Sunday morning sailed on one of Campbell's Steamers for Ilfracombe, calling everywhere on the way. I went with the skipper, Tom Welch, who was taking a short break at home, and we eventually arrived at Ilfracombe in the early afternoon, and with a bus to Braunton to enable me to dump my sea-bag, I made it to Fremington Camp with a few minutes to spare!

I completed an extended National Service in Christmas 1949, as with the Berlin Airlift and the possibility of war with Russia my period of service was lengthened by three months. I had been accepted for a public health course with Bristol Merchant Venturers starting in April 1950. In the intervening time I found work on a seaweed barge, the *"Dorothy"*, out of Braunton. The skipper was "young" Jan Crick of Braunton, the son of Jan Crick with whom I first ventured to sea in the *"Bessie."* He was a strong chap and had worked in most areas of coastwise sail and the gravel trades, together with motor ships etc – a good all-rounder.

21. The small seaweed barge "Dorothy"
Sam Mitchell

The *"Dorothy"* was used to collect seaweed, which was taken to Velator Quay, where it was dumped on the quayside for farmers to collect with tractors and trailers for use as fertiliser. This was principally used on the bulb farm at Braunton. At that time they would have truckloads of "shoddy" (factory waste from the carpet and textile industry), which was mixed with the seaweed and composted to improve the ground. They used to grow bulbs in sandy ground, that had very little nutrient at Braunton Bulb Farm. Hundreds of people worked at this location as the farm was very extensive. The manager was a Mrs. Snell, who was a tough egg. She could stand her ground very well. The seaweed barge had been built by Thomas Waters of Appledore many years before and had a small sail and auxiliary motor. It could carry around 5 tons on each trip and the seaweed would be ripped from the rocks with the barge being conned between the long gullies between the rocks until the tide ebbed and she took the ground, enabling the two crew to get over the side and to collect the weed. We would pull this from the rocks with our bare hands and gather the seaweed in heaps. The weed could be either loaded directly into the barge, or would be carried on a wooden stretcher and tipped into the barge.

When discharging the seaweed would be unloaded from the hold using traditional four-pronged dung-forks. Even though the cargo amounted to only around 5 tons each day, it

22. *"Result" entering Turf Lock, Exeter Canal around 1930 after delivering her cargo.*

was very hard work and a long 12-hour day for comparatively little reward. If we had sufficient time after loading the seaweed cargo, we would set off again to collect and bag mussels as the skipper had a lucrative ready market for these as a sideline. Whilst he operated the boat alone he would occasionally get assistance from a labourer, who might ride his bike down to where the seaweed was generally found, or, as with me, would accompany him down from Velator Quay and back. The seaweed barge would use the motor to go down Braunton Pill, but would use the sail to assist on the return passage. The vessel was rigged with a single loose-footed standing lugsail, which, with the prevailing southwesterly wind proved its worth in regaining Velator Quay. I worked in this trade from January to April 1950 when I went to the Merchant Venturers Technical College now a part of Bristol University.

In early September 1950 I was cycling through Braunton when Peter Welch hailed me and said he needed me aboard the *"Result"* which was to be used for a filming venture in the Scilly Isles. I said I could not go as I was on course for my final examinations, but he suggested I brought my books with me and joined them. Captain Tom Welch had by now passed on and Peter was her master. *"Result"* was at the time refitting at Appledore and having her topsail yards restored for filming, and they needed two additional hands, myself and Sid Crick. After some discussion at home and with some reservations, mainly from my mother, as I had already told Peter I would go, I joined the ship and stood by the *"Result"* at Appledore daily whilst the refit was in progress, and doing all sorts of minor jobs on the hull and gear as required. Four of us from Braunton would motor-sail to Appledore each day in Sid Crick's boat. Around ten days later we sailed from Appledore. Our crew consisted of Captain Peter Welch, the mate, Sam Mitchell, the A.B. Tom Slade, who had been a past master in the coasting sailer *"Margaret Hobley"*, Mickey Kemp from Ilfracombe as cook/boy, Sid Crick and myself. With Mickey I was responsible for handling the topsails when required. We initially sailed to Padstow as we did not like the look of the weather. I suspect Peter's intention was to drag out the passage for as long as possible, given he had been time-chartered, as no sooner had we got to St. Ives, that Peter decided the weather was not looking good and put into Hayle. The vessel was chartered for a rate of around £60 per day and was to be returned at the end of the filming restored to her original condition. Whilst in Padstow, where we stayed for a couple of days, we were visited by the film director Carol Reed.

23. *"Result" when filming as "Flash" in 1950, with (left to right) Sid Crick, Mickey Kemp, Sam Mitchell, Peter Welch (dressed as Captain Lingard) and Robert Andrew.*

We eventually got to St. Mary's, Isles of Scilly, where we were joined by a local pilot, Algie Guy, who remained aboard for the local filming over the period from the end of September 1950 and for most of October. I left half way through with Peter covering for me, whilst I took my final examinations and thereafter returned. We were in port every night and out for the day filming the "Outcast of the Islands." The vessel had been renamed *"Flash"* for the film and especially made name-boards were bolted over the name of the *"Result"* during the filming. Only one actor was aboard whilst we were filming – a stand-in for Trevor Howard who I do not think looked much like him at all! Peter Welch was given the part of Captain Lingard and remained master of the ship at all times. He was a very good likeness of the actor he stood in for. None of the real actors ever came on board and we never saw the young lady we were supposed to have rescued – despite our hopes! Everything else was filmed in the studio, done up to represent the East Indies. To assist we were all required to wear make up to colour our skin together with a sarong, apart from Tom Slade who absolutely refused and probably

24. "Result" when filming in 1950 as "Flash" in "Outcast of the Islands" seen in the Isles of Scilly - Peter Welch

would have continued to wear his trilby if permitted! We were paid an extra rate of £2.00 per day to clean off the "Max Factor" pancake mix that they coloured our skin with, in addition to the fixed rate of £10 per week, which was very good money in those days. We filmed around the Scillies calling at Tresco and many of the outlying islands. We did not have many strong winds, the weather being generally benign for the period. During this time I had made arrangements for a wire to be sent to St. Mary's harbourmaster to give my examination results – and was delighted to receive a brown Post Office telegraphed envelope with the one word "Pass" inside it!. Whilst staying over at St. Mary's the crew of *"Result"* became the champion dart players on the island – principally due to Sid Crick and Sam Mitchell. The film crew would film us from a motorboat and also had cameras set up on rocky islets and cliff sides at various locations where we were required to sail by. Generally whilst initially it was something of a novelty it soon began to pall, and we were all glad when this period finally came to an end and we returned to Appledore. We had carried the topsails all the way from the Scillies to Barnstaple Bay, before Mickey and I took in the topsails at around 2.00am off Hartland Point in the first day or so of November 1950.

About February 1951, Peter telephoned me. He was short-handed and asked if I could come for a trip. As a result I joined the *"Result"* at Ilfracombe and sailed across to Newport, where we loaded coal for Dunball on the Bridgewater River. We discharged our cargo in a day, before visiting the local hostelry – the "Green Man" – at Dunball, where we enjoyed our usual convivial evening. We thereafter returned to Ilfracombe where I left the ship, and rejoined the *"Dorothy"* at Velator.

Later in 1951 I secured a post as assistant public health inspector with South Molton Rural District Council. After a short period I had become totally disillusioned with the job and somewhat influenced by my future father-in-law, Skipper Jack Hamling with his stories of deep-sea fishing out of Hull. He lived at Fremington. His father had also been in deep-sea trawling and retired to Georgeham. Jack had gone to Chaloner's School at Braunton with my father and many other local boys. Dr. Chaloner had founded this school in 1667. Skipper Jack Hamling was taking a new trawler, the *"Arctic Warrior"* launched at Beverley in May 1951 by my future wife, on her maiden voyage of 19 days. I was invited to join the trawler and on Monday 9 July 1951, we landed 3,200 kit – equivalent to 250 tonnes - of cod at Hull. We had set out after the vessel was finally completed on Thursday 21 June. It was an interesting experience working 18 hours a day gutting, washing and stowing fish. If you reached the position of skipper or mate it could be a well-paid job, but I decided that it was not the life for me. We had sailed to the Norwegian Sea and fished for about 2 weeks around Bear Island. It was just continuous hard work. This was an important fishing ground and I recall counting the number of trawlers around us. There were over seventy from Russia, Finland, Norway, France and Britain - every European country you could think of. We were fishing in about 190 fathoms (about 347 metres). These fishing grounds were on the route of the convoys to Russia, and being well inside the Arctic Circle, in May it was almost continuously light. During our trawls we would occasionally bring up wreckage from the previous hostilities – pieces of aircraft etc.

On my return I went down to Bideford, looking for a ship. I saw a vessel alongside Bideford Quay, discharging coal; a flat bottomed vessel that had been mass-produced on the river Humber in 1942 and 1943, when some fifty-three ships had been launched at Goole. The ships had been constructed similarly to the "Liberty" ships, being assembled from 23 sections, welded together at Goole. Some were intended as tankers and some as cargo vessels, each with a capacity of around 500 tons. This class of vessel was designed to land stores on Normandy Beaches although the precise location of any invasion had not then been decided. Known as the *"Chant"* class they were 142.2ft. in length, 27.0ft. in beam with a depth of hold of 8.5ft., with a poop 42ft. in length, a central trunk 84ft. in length and a forecastle of 16ft. With a gross tonnage of 402 tons and a net of about 215 tons. The one I joined had been slightly modified by the skipper, Captain Griffin to carry 500 tons. He had been a deep-water skipper The Chant vessels were nicknamed "Churchill's Holy Answer to the Nazi Scourge". Captain Griffin was a very musical Welsh master who had a piano on board which he would play with gusto whilst waiting for his lunch.

He took me on as a very ordinary seaman aboard the *"Farringay"* as she was now named, and for our first passage together we departed from Bideford on 12 July 1951. She carried around eight crew: the skipper and mate, two engineers, a cook and around three deck crew, together with the skipper's wife. The principal cargo was coal for which Captain Griffith had a contract to supply the local gas works. We sailed to Port Talbot where we loaded carbide in drums for Fleetwood, which was a dangerous cargo with "no smoking" allowed. We arrived on the 15th. at Fleetwood from where we sailed up the Manchester Ship Canal to Partington coaling basin. We then brought coal to Bideford and always reckoned on taking 36-hours to sail from Mersey Bar to Bideford Bar. The ship had only a small 250hp Petter diesel engine which could push her along at a maximum of 8 knots in fair weather. The chief engineer was a Braunton man, George Ayres, whose grandfather had had the ketch *"Olive Branch"* which was well remembered in Braunton. He had a mass of spare parts on board for the engines and could probably have built a complete new engine from the pieces. I can remember going to Fleetwood and finding a similar vessel still waiting for spares whilst we had carried more than sufficient to take care of all repairs. He had a small motorcycle that he kept on board and once took me home on the pillion from Gloucester. The skipper had a three-wheeled car, which was kept in a special container on board and would be lifted by derrick onto the quayside as soon as we arrived in port, and he and his wife, who sailed with him, would go off to do the shopping. He would look upon his home port as being in Bideford.
Mrs Griffin was a very good helmsman and would often take the wheel, whilst the rest of us chipped paint on deck. I did a total of thirty-nine passages in the *"Farringay"* where we

worked seven days a week. I can recall discharging three cargoes in one week. As remuneration we were paid a fixed sum of £5.00 each week as "overtime", and with no timesheets you worked every hour of every day! The basic rate was in the order of £5.00 also, so the total was not bad for 1951 with all food included and lodging.

The passages we traded to included the following:

12.07.51	Bideford to Port Talbot	Light	13.07.51
14.07.51	Port Talbot to Fleetwood	Carbide	15.07.51
17.07.51	Fleetwood to Partington	Light	18.07.51
19.07.51	Partington to Bideford	Coal	20.07.51
22.07.51	Bideford to Lundy	Pontoons etc	

We unloaded the two pontoons by derrick and placed the trailer on board, before lifting the generator onto the trailer, whereupon a motor boat came off the island and towed the pontoons and their loads ashore.

22.07.51	Lundy to Avonmouth	Light	24.07.51
24.07.51	Avonmouth to Plymouth	Wheat	25.07.51
26.07.51	Plymouth to Newlyn	Light	27.07.51
27.07.51	Newlyn to Bristol	Stone chippings	28.07.51
30.07.51	Bristol to Avonmouth	Light	30.07.51
01.08.51	Avonmouth to Plymouth	Wheat	02.08.51
03.08.51	Plymouth/Dene Quarries	Light	04.08.51

Dene Quarries were situated inside the Manacles and were a tricky place to reach

04.08.51	Dene Quarries to Poole	Stone chippings	05.08.51
08.08.51	Poole to Par	Light	09.08.51
10.08.51	Par to Runcorn	China clay	

I left the vessel having loaded china clay at Par and had a few days off before rejoining the ship in Bideford.

	Runcorn to Partington	Light	
	Partington to Bideford	Coal	
20.08.51	Bideford to Newport	Light	21.08.51
21.08.51	Newport to Falmouth	Coal	22.08.51
24.08.51	Falmouth to Fowey	Light	24.08.51
27.08.51	Fowey to Runcorn	China clay	29.08.51
30.08.51	Runcorn to Partington	Light	30.08.51
01.09.51	Partington to Bideford	coal	02.09.51
05.09.51	Bideford to Swansea	light	05.09.51
06.09.51	Swansea to Belfast	coal	07.09.51
10.09.51	Belfast to Penmaenmawr	light	11.09.51

I remember a dense fog on this passage and we would sail for a mile and then stop, listen and proceed a further mile, before we would again stop and listen. We never saw the Isle of Man on this passage. The *"Farringay"* was not equipped with radar but only a small ship to shore radio.

11.09.51	Penmaenmawr/Liverpool	Stone chippings	11.09.51
12.09.51	Liverpool/Penmaenmawr	Light	13.09.51
13.09.51	Penmaenmawr/Liverpool	Stone chippings	13.09.51
14.09.51	Liverpool to Partington	Light	14.09.51
14.09.51	Partington to Bideford	Coal	16.09.51
17.09.51	Bideford to Swansea	Light	17.09.51
18.09.51	Swansea to Gloucester	Coal briquettes	19.09.51
24.09.51	Gloucester to Swansea	Light	25.09.51

26.09.51	Swansea to Garston	Coal briquettes	27.09.51
28.09.51	Garston to Partington	Light	29.09.51
01.10.51	Partington to Bideford	Coal	03.10.51
03.10.51	Bideford to Swansea	Light	03.10.51
04.10.51	Swansea to Garston	Coal briquettes	05.10.51
09.10.51	Garston to Partington	Light	09.10.51
10.10.51	Partington to Bideford	Coal	12.10.51

I paid off the *"Farringay"* on the 13 October 1951 and then joined the *"Result"* for the last time.

5. The ss "Farringay" seen under the port quarter of the "Result" at Appledore, August 1956
courtesy Hugh Thomas

Peter Welch had fallen between the ship and the quayside at St. Helier and had broken his leg and was in hospital for many months. He was replaced by Captain Tom Slade, who previously had been working aboard as AB. I had heard from home from the nominal owner, Captain Harry Clarke, that they were in need of a hand. I caught the next boat to Jersey from Weymouth and joined the ship around the 14 October. When I got to the ship the two crew, Sam Mitchell and Tom Slade went on holiday for a week and left me to look after the ship. On their return we loaded coal dust in St. Helier for St. Samson's and sailed on the 19th. October and arrived the same day.

A schedule of her passages is as follows:

19.10.51	St Helier/St. Sampsons	Coal dust	19.10.51

20.10.51	St Sampsons/St. Helier	Light	20.10.51
10.11.51	St Helier/St. Sampsons	Coal dust	10.11.51
13.11.51	St Sampsons to Eling	Stone chippings	14.11.51

Eling is a small port on the Solent, and we sailed from there to Northam, near Southampton

	Eling to Northam	Light	
23.11.51	Northam to Swansea	Baled scrap iron	27.11.51

We ran into gales of wind and were two days anchored at Jack-in-the-Basket in the Western Solent off Lymington taking shelter. We had 6 lengths of chain on the anchor (over 500 feet) and it took a month of Sundays to haul it all back, as the winch had failed.

29.11.51	Swansea to Gloucester	coal briquettes	30.11.51

We used the Sharpness and Gloucester Canal for these trips. There are fifteen bridges that had to be opened over the length of the canal.

04.12.51	Gloucester to Swansea	Wheat	06.12.51
10.12.51	Swansea to Gloucester	Coal briquettes	12.12.51
14.12.51	Gloucester to Swansea	Wheat	15.12.51
18.12.51	Swansea to Gloucester	Coal briquettes	20.12.51

We then had a Christmas break tied up in Gloucester Docks and we all went home for the holiday.

04.01.52	Gloucester to Sharpness	Light	04.01.52
05.01.52	Sharpness to Barry	Wheat	05.01.52
08.01.52	Barry to Avonmouth	Light	08.01.52
18.01.52	Avonmouth to Swansea	Wheat	18.01.52

On our passage this run we encountered a north-north-westerly gale, but still got in the same day

19.01.52	Swansea to Ilfracombe	Light	19.01.52
20.02.52	Ilfracombe to Swansea	Light	20.02.52
22.02.52	Swansea to Gloucester	Coal briquettes	23.02.52
25.02.52	Gloucester to Swansea	Light	26.02.52
27.02.52	Swansea to Gloucester	Coal briquettes	03.03.52
04.03.52	Gloucester to Ely	Light	05.03.52
06.03.52	Ely to Ilfracombe	Coal	06.03.52
12.03.52	Ilfracombe to Lydney	Light	12.03.52
14.03.52	Lydney to Ilfracombe	Coal	14.03.52
18.03.52	Ilfracombe to Ely	Light	18.03.52
19.03.52	Ely to Ilfracombe	Coal	19.03.52
21.03.52	Ilfracombe to Lydney	Light	22.03.52
22.03.52	Lydney to Ilfracombe	Coal	23.03.52
26.03.52	Ilfracombe to Lydney	Light	26.03.52
27.03.52	Lydney to Ilfracombe	Coal	27.03.52
01.04.52	Ilfracombe to Ely	Light	01.04.52
02.04.52	Ely to Ilfracombe	Coal	02.04.52
08.04.52	Ilfracombe to Lydney	Light	08.04.52
09.04.52	Lydney to Ilfracombe	Coal	10.04.52
22.04.52	Ilfracombe to Swansea	Light	22.04.52
23.04.52	Swansea to Gloucester	Coal briquettes	24.04.52
29.04.52	Gloucester to Avonmouth	Light	29.04.52
09.05.52	Avonmouth to Barry	Wheat	09.05.52
09.05.52	Barry to Avonmouth	Light	09.05.52
14.05.52	Avonmouth to Swansea	Wheat	15.05.52
16.05.52	Swansea to Avonmouth	Light	16.05.52
28.05.52	Avonmouth to Barry	Wheat	28.05.52

29.05.52	Barry to Avonmouth	Light	29.05.52
07.06.52	Avonmouth to Swansea	Barley	07.06.52
09.06.52	Swansea to Appledore	Light	10.06.52

As we ran over the Bar we ran into a thick fog. Tom Slade was on the wheel and immediately spun the helm and went out on a reciprocal course. We stayed outside until within the hour the fog had cleared and we could safely enter. The following day on the 11 June *"Result"* entered dry dock for her Lloyd's Survey and the mate, Sam Mitchell and I spent the next few days tarring the whole of the bottom of the vessel. I paid off on the 21st. June 1952.

26. *"Result" in New Quay dry dock, June 1952 with Robert Andrew under her bows having completed tarring the hull with Sam Mitchell.*
    Courtesy Sam Mitchell

By this time I had come to the conclusion that I had to get a proper job ashore as cargoes were fast diminishing with the Bristol Channel trade dying away completely. Peter Welch returned to the vessel and took her out of the dry dock, but trading conditions had worsened and thereafter he generally traded along the south coast and to Jersey. Not much work was required to enable her to pass her Survey as she was generally kept in excellent order.

After working for a few months as a timber specialist with a Plymouth company I became employed by Greenwich Council in their Public Health department. However the Lynmouth Disaster intervened and Devon County Council were seeking surveyors and engineers to assist in the rebuilding of the town, and I joined them. I stayed with Devon County Council until my retirement as Roads Engineer and never again went back to commercial sail, being content to sail my yacht in the Exe estuary and, with my friends much larger yacht, sailing around the Brittany coast and Ireland.

3. THE STORY OF THE "*RESULT*"

BY TOM WELCH

27. "Result" as a topsail schooner in 1895 – Michael Bouquet

The schooner *"Result"* was built of steel at Paul Rogers' Yard in Carrickfergus, Northern Ireland to the order of Thomas Ashburner & Co, who were well-known schooner owners from Barrow-in-Furness. Her design was evolved at a series of meetings between Paul Rogers, her builder, Captain Robert Wright, the master of the Ashburner's schooner, *"Useful"*, and Mr. Richard Ashburner, a naval architect. The requirement was for the vessel to be a three-masted topsail schooner, designed to be of shallow draft, speedy, to sail without ballast and to be graceful in appearance. She was laid down in 1892 and launched in 1893. The shipyard had changed hands whilst the *"Result"* was on the blocks. Paul Rodgers had financial problems and the yard was taken over, the *"Result"* being completed by Robert Kent & Co.

Captain Robert Wright left the *"Useful"* and took command of the *"Result"*, and sailed her in the coastal and Irish Sea trades. It is said she was initially launched carrying double topsails, with a flying topgallant sail set above these on the foremast, but this must not have suited her, with her relatively shallow draft of 9ft. 6-inches (2.9 metres) aft, as soon after her launch the flying topgallant sail was discarded, and her three lower masts reduced in height by several feet.

28. "Result at Pill's Mouth, Velator Creek as a topsail schooner – Tom Welch

In 1909 the Ashburner brothers, Thomas and Richard decided to retire and sold their schooner fleet at a Public Auction at Connah's Quay, Cheshire. The *"Result"* was purchased by a group of seamen and investors from Braunton in north Devon, amongst them, Captain Henry Clarke, and Captain Sidney J. Incledon, who took command of her from Captain Wright at Sandwich in Kent in July 1907. My grandfather, Thomas Welch, joined her about a month later as mate – aged 19 years. – at Prince Regent's Wharf, London, loading railway sleepers for Highbridge, Somerset. After this change of ownership the vessel continued working in the coastal trade carrying all manner of cargoes: clay, coal, manure, bricks, etc.

In 1914 an auxiliary engine was installed at Appledore, a 45hp. Semi-diesel Kromhaust, but she retained her full rig.

In November 1916 the *"Result"* was requisitioned by the Government for use as a "Q-ship", and was sent to Lowestoft for refit. Ballasted with 100 tons of sand, she was filled with armaments, two 18 cwt. 12-pounder guns and torpedoes. During this time she was commissioned HMS *"Q-23"* and for a short time as a part disguised vessel renamed *"Dag"*. She made several sorties into the North Sea towards Dogger Bank under the command of Lieutenant P. J. Mack, R.N., with Lieutenant G. H. P. Mulhauser as second in command. She fought two actions, one with the German submarine *"U-45"* on the 15th. March 1917 and again on the 5th April 1917 with an unknown submarine.

The *"Result"* returned to her merchantman duties in March 1918 and resumed work in the coastal trade. This included several cargoes of coal from Cardiff to Morlaix in Brittany, which carried very high freights owing to the threat of U-boats and the number of merchant ships having been lost to them.

29. "Result" as HMS "Q23"

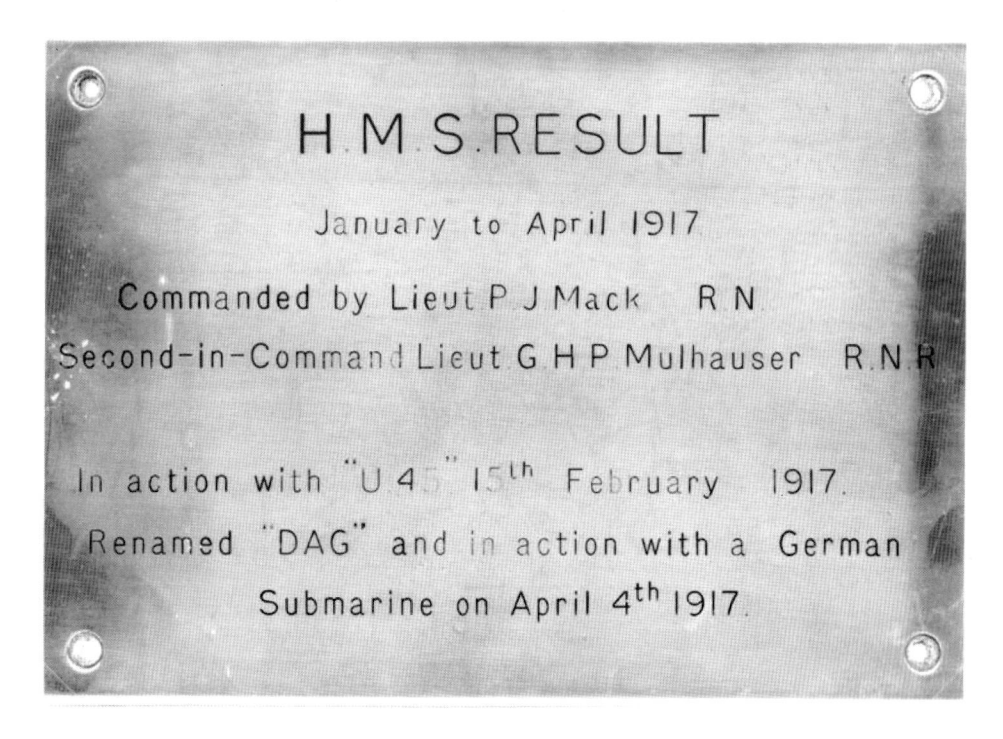

H.M.S. RESULT

January to April 1917.

Commanded by Lieut P J Mack   R N.

Second-in-Command Lieut G H P Mulhauser   R.N.R

In action with "U 45" 15th February 1917.

Renamed "DAG" and in action with a German Submarine on April 4th 1917.

30. "Result" – her record as a "Q" ship in 1917.

31. The Bill of Sale for 16 shares in the "Result" which were transferred from Susan Incledon, the wife of Captain Incledon, to Francis Ann Welch the wife of the ship's master on 25 June 1923 for £600. It will be noted the witness was Captain N. Heath of "Heathbank", Braunton, the name of one of Andrew Weir & Co.'s barques, which disappeared in 1900.

32. "Result" off Beachy Head in 1922 laden with Portmadoc slate bound for Amsterdam. Photo taken from a British Rail steamer proceeding from Newhaven to Le Havre.
Courtesy – Robert Andrew

33. "Result" seen light at Velator at the top of a spring tide pre-1939. One can see the top of a pile of gravel on the quayside where a barge has just completed discharging – Tom Welch

34. "Result" at Asham, 1936 – the late Bill Cook

35. "Result" lying in Ilfracombe in 1952 – Peter Welch

In the next period of her life, the 1920s, whilst still trading as a topsail schooner *"Result"* gained her reputation, narrated by Dr. Basil Greenhill in his book The Merchant Schooners, as "amongst the fastest and most useful schooners that ever sailed in home waters."

Captain Incledon retired in 1920 and my grandfather came from the ketch *"Democrat"* to become master of the *"Result"*. Under his command the sail plan was gradually altered over the years, at first to a fore-and-aft schooner with the removal of the square yards.

36. "Result" at Jersey in the 1950s – Tom Welch

37. "Result" when filming in 1950 as "Flash" in "Outcast of the Islands" seen in the Isles of Scilly - Peter Welch

38. The "Result" as the schooner "Flash", when filming "The Outcast of the Islands"
Robert Andrew

In 1946 a larger engine was installed: a 120hp. Widdop; also the hatch coamings were enlarged to facilitate cargo handling, and the wheelhouse was added..

Tom Welch died in 1948 and my father, Peter Welch took command. Father traded the *"Result"* on the South Coast to the Channel Islands and France. In 1950 she was re-

39. Ketch "Garlandstone" (left) and the "Result" at Big Quay, Velator – Tom Welch

rigged at Appledore as a topsail schooner and chartered to a film company. She was engaged in filming around the Scilly Isles for the film "Outcast of the Islands" under the name *"Flash"*. Once the filming was over she returned to Appledore, the topsail yards were sent down and she resumed her trading on the South Coast.

40. The 3-masted schooner "Result" leaving Solva – Tom Welch

41. "Result" leaving Solva, rounding St. David's Head

About 1955 the mainmast was removed in order that cargoes could be worked more easily and the *"Result"* continued trading as a motor ketch to the Channel Islands until the death of Peter Welch in 1967, when she returned to Exeter to be laid up with her blue band of mourning painted around the hull. She was later sold to the Ulster Folk Museum near Belfast, to be used as a static museum exhibit, where she remains.

Masters of the *"Result"*:

Robert Wright	1893 – 1909
Sidney John Incledon	1909 – 1921
Thomas Clarke Welch	1921 – 1948
Peter Russan Welch	1948 – 1967

I was born in Braunton in 1950 and first went to sea aged 9 with my father Peter Welch on his motor ketch *"Result"*, joining the vessel in Plymouth where she was loaded with bagged lime for Guernsey. In Guernsey we loaded stone chippings for Shoreham. I stayed aboard the vessel sleeping in the "locker" in my father's cabin "back aft", for about a fortnight, during which time we did two more trips to Guernsey. The mate was Ernie Stribling from Barnstaple, the cook "Uncle" Jim Endicott from Jersey and the A.B., was Ted Lenox, also from Jersey. The crew were very kind to a young boy and I ate forward with them in the fo'c'sle.

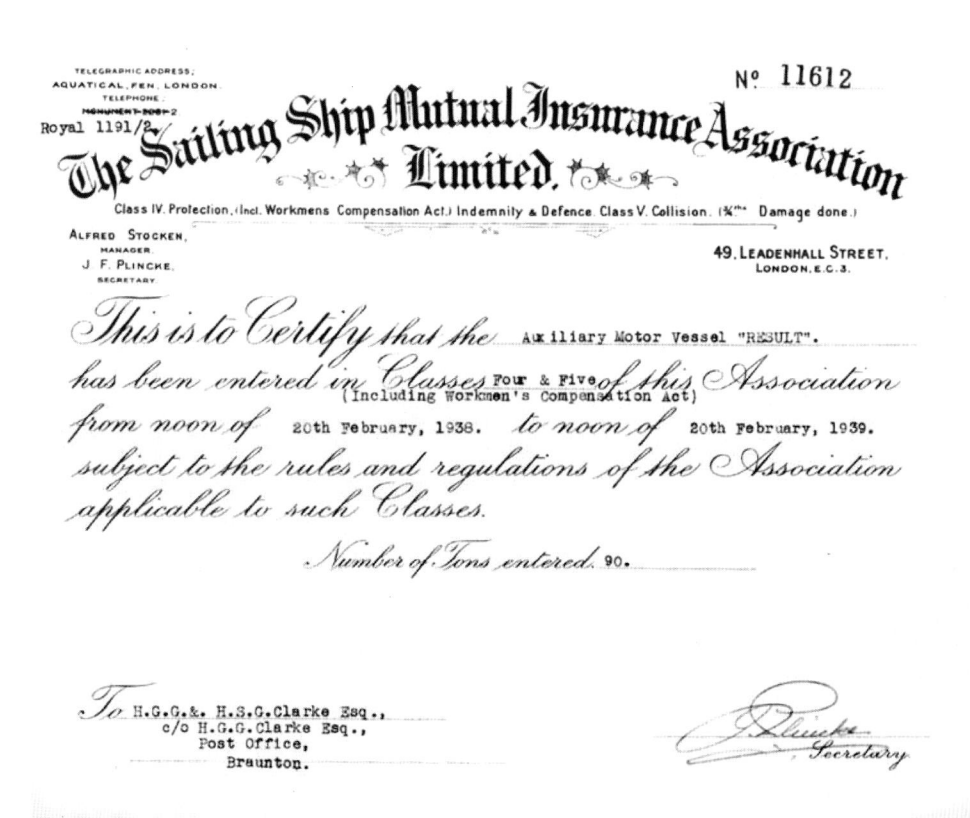

42. An insurance certificate for the "Result"

43. "Result" as a topsail schooner, at Stanbury's Mill, Barnstaple.

44. Early 1960s, "Result" now a two-masted ketch, discharging coal, at Tresco, Scilly
Peter Welch

45. "Result" rounding Land's End - © Richards Bros, Penzance

After that first trip I sailed for several summer holidays on the *"Result"*, often with my whole family, father and mother, my sister Sarah and brother Peter. The mate on these trips was Jan Crick from Velator, Braunton, with whom I had made a lot of trips at weekends in the 1960s, when he had been master of the former sailing, but then motor barge *"Hilda"*, fetching gravel from various banks on the Taw Estuary: Crow, North Bank, Sprat Ridge and Conigar, back to the quay at Velator.

In 1967 I became an indentured apprentice with the Bank Line Ltd., owned by Andrew Weir & Co. I joined the m.v. *"Levernbank"*, 8,500 grt in Hong Kong and stayed on her for 15 months and 15 days, my first voyage at £19 per month! The vessel was trading with general cargo from Far Eastern ports to East and South Africa. The Scottish-based Bank Lane had a fleet of about 50 vessels tramping worldwide. I later sailed on the m.v. *"Beechbank"* and then m.v. *"Hollybank"*, on which ship I became 3rd Mate, trading from the UK/Continent to Houston and the Gulf, through the Panama Canal to Australia. The homeward trip saw us loading copra, cocoa and coffee beans from the New Guinea islands back to the UK/Continent.

I obtained my 2nd Mate's certificate in 1972, and then sailed as 3rd Mate on the m.v. *"Teviotbank"* to India and East Africa, then 2nd Mate on the m.v. *"Willowbank"* and m.v.*"Forresbank"* up to the Baltic. I joined the m.v. *Sand Wyvern"* as Mate in 1974, a 500-ton dredger working from Plymouth to Hayle, Padstow and Bideford. We also made a few trips from Porthoustock Quarry near the Helford River with stone to rock quay, Cowes, I.o.W. or Whitstable in Kent. I stayed on the dredger about 12 months, then joined Offshore Marine, a Yarmouth company operating oil rig support vessels in the

46. The mv "Polar Bear" supply ship to Lundy Island

North Sea, working as Mate on a number of their ships: *"Arctic Shore", "Shetland Shore",* and *"Channel Shore",* quite a lot of the time from Aberdeen or Lerwick. A very rough job in winter with not much daylight!

I joined the *"Polar Bear"* as Mate at Ilfracombe in 1978, taking cargo and passengers to Lundy Island and remained on her for eight years until I "swallowed the anchor" in 1986.

47. The crew of the "Result" about 1936: (left to right): Peter Welch, Tom Welch, 'Smuggler' Hall and Peter Russan - Courtesy Tom Welch

4. THE SAND AND GRAVEL TRADE

ROBERT D'ARCY ANDREW AND DAVID CLEMENT

48. Sailing barges loading in the early 1900s. – David Clement Collection

THE BARGES:

The sand and gravel trade with Braunton and Appledore vessels taking material from the bars at the entrance to the estuary dates back to at least the Middle Ages, and information is recorded from the 1400s, as where three men were drowned in 1331 whilst putting stones alongside the Long Bridge at Barnstaple *'from a small barge.'* In the early days the vessels were essentially lighters, which doubled as sand barges when the need required, and later these same vessels served the pottery trade to Barnstaple, Fremington and Bideford. Such vessels would have been around 30 feet (9.5 metres) in length, and carrying up to 25 tonnes of gravel.

From the mid 19th century the trade grew significantly with the gravel being used for construction purposes. This was often associated with the dock development in the South Wales ports, with material being taken from the Crow, Middle Ridges, Klondike and Zulu banks.

The early barges were essentially sailed or poled to and from the banks relying very much on the tides to assist their progress. The vessels were based at Barnstaple,

49. A wintry scene with two barges passing down the river Taw from Barnstaple to collect gravel in the early years of the 20th. century
Photo courtesy of Stephen Knight of Barnstaple.

Bideford, and Appledore with some at Braunton. They were of traditional timber construction designed similar to the wooden coasting vessels and generally had 2½-inch outside planking with 1½-inch planking, known as the ceiling, inside the frames. The 19th century vessels were around 30 feet long by 13 feet beam, with a straight bow, sweet transom stern, and built largely of pitch pine or larch planking outside, with larch planking inside, and with an oak keel. These barges were built largely at Appledore or Bideford with the occasional vessel built at Barnstaple. Goss built one or two at Calstock on the river Tamar. They were generally sloop rigged with a pretty square mainsail with very little peak and a single foresail. Because they very rarely ventured outside the Bar they did not carry much spare canvas. As designed the barges had very little sheer. Most of the barges continued under sail until the early 1920s, but by 1930s most had engines. After the 1939-45 War mechanical loading using grabs on some barges was introduced.

The barges were owned by Bartletts of Bideford, Rock Trading Co (Rawle Gammon & Baker), of Barnstaple and Devon Trading Co. These were all essentially Builders Merchants. In Barnstaple to the 1950s R Harris, who were big building contractors, also owned barges. The Braunton Sand & Gravel Company had two wooden barges called *"Sixty Spec"* and *"Hilda,"* and later two steel barges were built for them called *"Busy Bee"* and *"R.H."* ("R. Harris"). The connection with their principal customer is clear! A unique one-man band was Jack Pile of Braunton, who owned his own barge. He initially had the *"JJRP"* built by Waters of Irsha Street, Appledore in 1923. Her measurements were 37 feet x 13 feet x 5 feet 4 inches, and she loaded 27 tons of gravel. *"JJRP"* were the initials of original owner – John and Julie Rapson Pile. This vessel was eventually sold to Saunders of Barnstaple, and later to Fred Mitchell of Braunton in 1949. He ran her till 1961 when she was laid up Braunton Pill until 1963.

50. Barges off Appledore Quay and waiting to go at 8.30am., June 2 1954 - seen from the deck of "Flower" are left to right, "Result", "Paul & Michael", the ketch "Maud Mary", with the "Princess Maysie" just visible in front, and the "Julie Pile" alongside to starboard.

51. Bound out – "Result" and the barge "Paul and Michael"
Both pictures from the David Clement Collection

47

52. Barges at Klondike, near Bideford Bar preparing to anchor, left to right "Result with the grab, the "Flower", "A.C.M." and the "Julie Pile" in June 1954.
David. Clement Collection

53. Anchors down and waiting to dry out on the gravel banks 2 June 1954 – left to right, "Marie", " and "Result" seen from the deck of the "Nellie"
David Clement Collection

She was towed to Bideford-East-the-Water by the *"Sixty-Spec"* where vandals set fire to her. The old barge was sunk to put out flames. She was later purchased by the North Devon Museum Trust, at Appledore in hopes of restoration. Having sold the *"JJRP,"* Jack Pile had the barge *"Julie Pile"* built by P. K. Harris of Appledore in 1925, measuring just 17 tons gross, 10 tons net. He would sell gravel to various contractors, taking the gravel to where they wanted – Bideford/Appledore/Barnstaple and a few barge loads to Braunton. The material was all used in the building trade and construction projects by the 20th century, but earlier in the $14^{th}/16^{th}/17th$ centuries the gravel may well have been used additionally for agricultural purposes – particularly the finer gravels, also known as "sea sand."

The barges rarely went outside the middle ridges. Klondike and Zulu banks were the farthest they ever went to seaward. This was inside the Bar across the estuary and was a part of the South Tail, which with North Tail lay just inside the bar to the estuary. The quality of the gravel got finer the further in but I do not remember them taking material from New Quay Ridge or Instow Sands as these may have been worked out by the time I was a boy. The other banks were worked until the end. This section was known locally as Shit-ass Bank. Sprat Ridge, opposite Appledore, was used till the last, together with Crow, to which it was linked.

The crew only had two to three hours between tides to load the gravel. The barges carried only two crewmembers and had to put 15 tonnes in each in the interval, generally working at a rate of five tons per hour. A full load could be got in the period between the tides from Pages Pill. Gravel was loaded using a shovel with a large traditional "D" shaped blade lifting around 25lbs for each shovel-full and throwing it up over one's shoulder, over the low deck rail directly into the hold. Loading would be done from the most advantageous side given the height and slope of the bank with the cargo being trimmed after the tide started to make. On the level the barge could be loaded from both sides. There are still men in Braunton who remember loading the barges – such as Sam Mitchell, who worked for his uncle Fred Mitchell, who owned his own barge, the *"JJRP"* as detailed above.

The operating pattern of the barges was that they would come down on the ebb tide from wherever they had taken the last cargo the previous day and take the ground on whichever bank they had chosen to work. The barge would be run up on the bank as far up as they could get as the tide dropped. As soon as it was shallow enough the two-man crew would throw over shovels and, wearing boots, would start to load the sandy gravel. The coarsest gravel was found at the Klondike/Zulu banks; this material was very heavy. The lightest gravel was at Crow or Sprat Ridge. There two men to each barge would load for about three to four hours maximum. The crew would take the anchor aboard before they had finished loading, and when all was ready and they were waiting upon the tide for "lift-off" tea would be made. The accommodation consisted of a small cuddy up forward. This was a very tight space with a small coal stove, where they could make hot tea, and or a fry-up etc. The cuddy was very cramped for sleeping and so the crew did not generally sleep on board overnight. As the tide rose, the crew trimmed and levelled the cargo; put the wooden hatches on; and covered this with tarpaulin sheets properly wedged in place with wood wedges hammered into place with a maul. Then they would sit and wait for the vessel to float free. The tide would now be making, or rising, fast. It is well known that during the 3rd and 4th hours of a tide, half of the tidal height is gained. Occasionally a barge would "suck" or stick to the bottom and

54. Barges loading – with "Paul & Michael", "Julie Pile", and the "Flower"

55. Barges loading at Klondike, June 1954, with "ACM", "Result" just visible over the bows, "Paul & Michael" the "Julie Pile" and beyond "the "Princess Mayse".
Both pictures from the David Clement Collection

56. Looking from Klondike, towards Appledore from the "Nellie" (foreground) with "Julie Pile", "Flower" (almost hidden), "Paul & Michael" and "Rowena" in the distance, with the "ACM" on the right. David Clement Collection

the only way to help free the vessel was to rock it if possible. It could be held fast and sink on occasions. The barge, if all went well, would suddenly float free with the tide, and, as she lifted, the engine would be started. Most of the barges had a 2-cylinder Widdops hot-bulb-semi-diesel engine. Other engines favoured were made by Kelvin or Kromhaust. In the days of sail, the jib would be raised with the mainsail scandalised until the vessel had floated free, when course would be set, aided by the tide. A motorised barge would turn on the tide and was then steered into the channel and proceeded to its destination. The freeboard of the vessel would only be a couple of inches, with the deck almost awash. As she passed through the salt water to the fresher water of the river, the barge would lie deeper until half the deck would be awash with the stern and cuddy just out of water. The crew relied on the hatch covers being watertight. They had to be careful not to overload the vessel – particularly on Klondike or Zulu banks, as the gravel there was very heavy.

The Barge was taken to its destination alongside a quay where the cargo was discharged. Before the Second World War they often unloaded alongside steamships where buckets would be lowered to the crew to load and be swung up to discharge into vessel. Cranes were similarly used at quaysides until grabs were introduced to ease unloading. Braunton, where it was discharged just above Big Quay, was always a hand discharge place, with no grabs. The crew of the barge threw sand/gravel onto the quayside, which was awash at high water. This was protected by timber planking to prevent material being washed back into the channel. Unloading the barge usually took

57. Flood tide coming in with "Julie Pile", "Flower", "Paul & Michael", "Rowena" and "ACM" seen from aboard "Nellie" with the crew of the latter getting in the anchor.

58. Almost Afloat – with "Nellie", "PKH", "Result", with the dinghy of the "Flower" in the foreground.
Both pictures from the David Clement Collection

59. Waiting to float off – aboard the "Nellie", with the "Julie Pile", and the "Paul & Michael" ahead. David Clement Collection

place in the evening and often a Third Hand, who had usually been working as a builder's labourer during the day, was employed to assist.

The heyday of barges was the period from 1870 to 1914, when much of the gravel was used for building docks developing along the Severn estuary at Avonmouth, Lydney, Newport, Swansea, Cardiff, Penarth, Barry, Port Talbot etc. Vast quantities were taken by small steamers, such as the *"Devonia"* built in 1894 at Irvine, and owned by the Bideford & Bristol Steamship Co. Ltd, of Bridgland Street, Bideford. She was an iron vessel, 85 feet x 18.1 feet x 7.5 feet, and only 38 tons net/99 tons gross with a 20hp steam engine driving a screw. A sister ship, the *"Roma"* was also built.

Another vessel served by the barges was the steamship *"Torridge"* built in 1904 by Robert Cock & Sons at Appledore. She was 158 tons gross/51 tons net, and measured 96.9 feet x 19.3 feet x 9.1 feet. She was built to carry gravel to Avonmouth, and carried the cargo of six or more barges loaded alongside. She was under the managing ownership of James Cock.

In bad weather the carrying of gravel in the barges was a risky business. As late as Friday 28 February 1959, two men, William Moore and Robert Patience, were swept overboard and drowned from *"Nellie Anne"* in an accident also involving *"ACM"*.[1] They

---

[1] The resultant legal claim by the estates of the deceased against William Gould & Co of Barnstaple (the owners of the *"Nellie Ann"*) and their employer's insurers, the Commercial

60. Getting afloat – "Princess Mayse" with her Bartletts grab crane, and the "Result".

61. Returning with the "Maud Mary", "Paul & Michael" and "Princess Mayse"
Both pictures from the David Clement Collection

Union Assce. Co. Ltd, and the insurers of the ACM Gravel Co. the owners of the "*A.C.M*" (also the Commercial Union Assurance Co. Ltd.) was amongst the first in which the writer was involved. William Moore was aged 51 years, married with a grown up son, whilst Robert Patience left a wife and two young children.

62. Deep laden, the "Paul & Michael" returns.

63. The barge "Marie" of Salcombe, now a gravel barge returning up the Torridge with sand in May 1951
Both photographs from the David Clement Collection

64. Gravel being unloaded from the sailing barge "Hilda" at Braunton Pill, with the quayside awash. Courtesy Bill Mitchell

65. Four barges discharging at Braunton – including the sailing barge "Hilda" in August 1943. The timber baffles on the quayside that prevented the hard-won cargo from being washed back into the channel at the top of the tide, can be clearly seen
Courtesy David B. Clement Collection

had been loading gravel at Middle Ridge, well inside the estuary and all three barges were anchored around 60 feet apart. The *Nellie H.* was the first to float away as the tide came in, with the *A.C.M.* needing another foot of water to float when the *Nellie Ann*, dragging her anchor, came towards them. The *Nellie Ann* floated close by the *A.C.M.*, which tried to manoeuvre out of the way, when the anchor rope of the *Nellie Ann* became fouled on the propeller of the *A.C.M.* and made it useless. The engine of the *Nellie Ann* was not operating and the crew of the *A.C.M.* were endeavouring to pull both vessels away on their engine, but without success, the vessels having become hemmed in against the bank. Distress signals were sent up and as both barges were forced to the top of the bank it was evident they were sinking, as neither barge could get clear, and the seas began to wash deck gear from both vessels. The crew of the *A.C.M.*, James Passmore and Fred Hill were rescued from the water by the Appledore pilot boat. The incident occurred by Zulu Bank, lying between the Bar Buoy, and Middle Ground buoy. At the time there was a heavy ground sea and a swift flowing tide resulting in broken water, which appears to have flooded both barges. The pilot boat was waiting for the collier *Pertinence* and seeing distress flares, saw the crews clinging to the exhaust stacks of both vessels and in difficulties. As the pilot boat went to their assistance all four crew were swept into the sea by a large wave, two of whom were carried alongside the pilot boat and rescued. The third barge on the bank, the *Nellie H.*, also with two crew aboard, managed to get off safely.

I remember Fred Mitchell working post war in the 1950s, and his nephew, Sam Mitchell, who was mate of the ketch *"Result"* for many years. The barge trade continued to the 1970s. The sailing barge, *Hilda,* was built by Waters of Appledore about 1927, and owned by Harry 'Blue' Mitchell of South Street, Braunton. *"Hilda"* was around to the late 1940s and was the last barge working under sail. A motor was installed towards the end. She was then sold to South Wales owners for use as a yacht. On the first attempt to take her over the bar two people were washed overboard and drowned.

The details of these gravel barges will not generally be found in the *Mercantile Navy List* or *Lloyd's Registers*, as the vessels always worked inside the bar and were classed as river vessels.

THE KETCHES:

As well as the small steamers, all sizes of ketch were used in the gravel trade, with the smallest taking only 60 tons. The *"Enid"*, for example, carried 65 tons. The largest carried 100 tons. Loading was carried out using a team of hobblers (or spare hands) – averaging six men to the team - shovelling the gravel into maunds or baskets. These could hold up to 5 cwts, and would be swung up onto the deck of the vessels and emptied into the hold. This was achieved on one tide using three or four maunds/baskets, the six men loading the baskets and the crew of the ketch swinging them up by using the vessel's winches – generally operated by hand, and emptying into the hold. The maunds were made at Braunton basket factory, which closed down around 1960.

The ketches would never load at Klondike or Zulu banks, but always at Crow or Sprat Ridge. They took their cargoes directly to the docks within the Severn estuary. The vessels did not normally sail on the same tide but generally waited until the following tide. The hobblers were hired by the day for perhaps two to three shillings (£0.10p./£0.15p.) to carry out the work. They would travel to the banks either aboard the ketch or on foot to Crow Point from where they would be collected by the ship's boat. Alternatively they could wait until the vessel took the ground when it was possible for them to walk out to her. The team of hobblers would be put ashore from the ketch's boat, and would then walk home from there, although if they judged it correctly they could also walk back across the flats to Crow Point as the tide made and thereafter walk home. The heyday of this trade was very much in the period of the dock developments along the South Wales coast. Though the trade had largely died by the 1920s, as dock development had more or less come to an end by then, Gordon Mote's book, *The Westcountrymen*, describes loading gravel aboard the ketch *"Enid"* as late as 1939. By this period the limited cargoes were generally used as a building or construction material to be mixed with cement in making concrete.

The vessels used in this way were principally ketches, although the occasional schooner might have loaded the odd cargo – or used the banks as a useful source of ballast when this was required. Most of the ketches, which were used in this trade, were from Braunton. These included besides the *"Enid"*, the *"Kitty Ann"*, *"Maud"* *"Bessie Gould"*, *"Bessie"* and *"Amazon"*. Not many vessels from Barnstaple or Appledore were engaged. There was very little money in this work as the freight on gravel was extremely low. It could be said that this was a true form of "sweated labour" as the work was extremely hard and the rewards were a pittance.

From the tonnages taken from the banks where the area was within the parish of Braunton, the local authority collected 1/- per ton from every barge and ketch. Most of the banks – Crow Point, Peaches Pill, (correctly Pages Pill) etc – were within this area, whilst Klondike and Zulu were within Northam Parish, and New Quay Ridge was partially in Instow/Westleigh parishes.

66. Loading in the 1940s – "ACM" and "Advance" off Crow Point

5. APPROACHING THE BAR

ROBERT D'ARCY ANDREW

BIDEFORD BAR

NAVIGATIONAL AIDS SINCE 1822

The entrance to the Taw and Torridge estuary lies between Northam and Braunton Burrows about 1½ miles offshore, and the channel, which often shifts, comprises a bar of coarse sand and gravel with extensive shoals or tails on either side. The South Tail, with a high patch of gravel known *as* Zulu Bank, and the North Tail with a lower gravel patch known as the Crumbles.

The bar itself is very shallow with a depth of only 3ft (1 metre) at low water springs. The seabed shoals rapidly up to the bar from a depth of 40ft (13 metres) at the Fairway Buoy and the shallow area extends for nearly a mile with deeper water inside.

Navigation in the estuary has always been subject to the restriction of the shallow bar at the mouth, a major problem, with the addition of a fearsome reputation that in strong westerly winds the heavy groundswell turns the bar area into a maelstrom of breaking seas. In the closing days of sail in N. Devon - now almost lost to memory - with sailing vessels equipped with auxiliary power it was still the practice when running the bar in heavy weather for two strong men to be roped at the wheel and the rest of the crew to climb into the rigging to avoid being washed off the deck in the event of the vessel becoming pooped.

The flood tide sweeps into the bay around Hartland Point and into the estuary with in addition a strong tidal set occurring across the entrance in a N.N.E direction. In the days of sail in the event of a vessel endeavouring to run the bar in a strong westerly wind with heavy groundswell it ran the risk of being 'pooped and broaching to' and becoming generally overwhelmed. With this tidal set the vessel would invariably end up ashore wrecked on the North Tail.

To enable ships to proceed over the bar in greater safety and also to enter by night as well as by day leading lights were installed in 1822, being set at a distance of 933ft (306 metres) apart. The upper or inner lighthouse was a white tower 85ft (27.9 metres) high, and could always be seen at 14 miles (22.5 kms.) from a vessel's deck. The lower lighthouse was a cubic wooden structure also white, so placed on a frame as to allow it to be moved northward or southward, to preserve the line of the two lights right through the channel, according to the shift of the sands. The lantern of the lower light was 40ft above high water and visible from 11 miles (17.7 kms.).

67. Braunton Higher Light showing sailing vessels beating out over the Bar. The Tide Ball, marking half flood, which was raised adjacent to the Low Light when it was safe to cross the Bar, can be seen to the left of the Lighthouse. The smaller building further to the left was the Low Light, the two lights being about 933ft. (306 metres) apart. The lighthouse was divided into two semi-detached homes for the Keeper and his assistant and their families. They were responsible for all three lights and ensuring they were supplied with paraffin every day or so. This photo was taken around 1900. – Courtesy Braunton Museum.

Sailing directions in the 19th century advised mariners not to enter before 1/2 flood when 15ft. (4.9 metres) of water should be present over the bar. By day this was indicated by the raising of a large black wickerwork ball on a staff placed between the light towers from half flood to half ebb. At night the low light showed red from ½ ebb to ½ flood and changed to white from ½ flood to ½ ebb when it was considered safe to enter with a minimum of 15ft (4.9 metres) of water over the bar. Unlit starboard hand buoys also indicated the channel direction.

The high light was of timber construction clad in oak shingles, the house below was of stone and brick construction and housed two keepers and their families. Close at hand were chicken and pig houses together with a mortuary with capacity for about a dozen bodies placed around the sides on Delabole slate slabs raised 2ft above the floor, rather like an old dairy. For the benefit of vessels outward bound and equally to alert the keeper on duty a goal post like structure was placed at the edge of the channel close to the high light. This indicated ½ flood when the cross bar went under water.

68. The Higher Light showing the half-tide mark directly in front on the foreshore. When the horizontal beams were covered there was sufficient water to cross the Bar.- a minimum of 15ft. (4.9 metres) – Courtesy Braunton Museum.

*69. A fine aerial photograph of the High Light looking across the estuary towards Westward Ho! by E. A. Sweeting & Sons Ltd of Tonbridge Wells
David Clement Collection*

70. Braunton Low Light showing the Tide Ball, which marked half flood, with the two pulley wires to enable this to be raised when required. The Ball was lowered and housed within the black box, or 'keeper', seen at its base when not in use. The structure of the light and rails were made of pitch-pine and enabled the light to be positioned to the left/right, dependent upon the changes in the channel from the Bar. All of these navigation aids were removed in 1957, when the lights were reinstated at Instow. The photo shows the late Verbena Ford and is courtesy Ann Wells, née Ford.

Captain Denham the naval officer who first charted the estuary in 1832 states in sailing directions published in 1859: -

"DIRECTIONS FOR SAILING OVER THE BAR - Ships in stormy weather, with the wind on any point between N.N.W. and W.S .W., should take care to have the lights, or towers in one when they enter the breakers, as the stream of flood sets strong across the entrance toward N.N.E.. By keeping the lights on, they will run in safety (when over the bar) to a fair berth off the Middle Ridge, which will show itself on the starboard hand; and they will probably obtain a pilot, if in the day-time, before they come near the outer light-tower, about 250 fathoms from which, with the lights still in one, the channel becomes very narrow, by reason of the S.E., or inner point of the Middle Ridge. At this point, and being still without a pilot, the lights should be gradually open to the westward, hauling over towards the Grey Sand-hills, south, or S. by W., with a flood-tide. Before getting the length of the stony beach at the southernmost point of those sand-hills, which is steep-to, it may be expected some assistance will be afforded to bring the vessel into a safe berth.

But if in desperate cases by night, in thick stormy weather, those who are entirely unacquainted, should, for the preservation of life, be constrained to run for the harbour, they have only to keep the lights in one, as before directed, until they approach the outer light to less than 200 fathom's distance; then opening the high light to the westward of the low light, hauling over to the southward, and passing both lights, they must act as circumstances may require for their preservation. Being now in comparatively smooth water, they will endeavour to run in as far as they can, taking care not to get on shore under the steep cliffs at the west end of the town of Appledore, because immediately under those cliffs the bottom is rocky, and many limestone heaps lie there; or they may continue their course past the stony beach at Grey Sand-hills, and run on shore on the mud at Skern. Abreast of Appledore is the Pool, which is 1/3 of a mile in length, by 11/2 cable wide; its depths are from 15 to 30 feet at low water. Here you may anchor as soon as Northam Church tower (a yellow square-towered building) comes on with the town, and Tapeley House (a conspicuous mansion about a mile S. by E. from Appledore, on the east side of Bideford Beach), is clearly open of the town. No stranger should proceed further without the assistance of a pilot."

Captain Denham then says, *"This pool is, however, a valuable stopping-place, whether bound in or out; and as the pilots in very severe weather, which is the time they are most required, are not to be found outside the bar, it is of the utmost importance to be able to take up, unassisted, the only sheltered anchorage within the bar. Further than Appledore none but coasters ought to proceed without a pilot, for the navigation of both Barnstaple and Bideford Rivers is rendered very intricate, not only from the shifting of the sands, but from the injurious position of certain weirs."*

About 1908 Bideford Bar Light, known locally as 'Blinking Billy', a steel fabricated structure, was installed immediately north of Airy point on the edge of the dunes with the purpose of providing cross bearings to the bar at night. It had two sectors of light, one white directed at the bar buoy and one red directed at the middle ridge buoy. A vessel running the bar on the leading lights traversed through the white sector, and immediately on leaving it the bar buoy would be seen on the starboard bow. Continuing on the leading lights and passing through the red sector of Bideford Bar Light, immediately on leaving it the middle ridge buoy would be seen on the starboard bow. The vessels course would then be gradually altered to starboard in a South Easterly direction towards the two Pulley Buoys and on to Sprat Ridge Buoy leading into Appledore Pool. At the outbreak of war in 1939 Bideford Bar Light was extinguished and finally in 1946 it was abandoned. In 1957 the high light became unsafe and was removed and a steel lattice tower erected in its place. Shortly afterwards the High and Low lights were removed and erected on shore at Instow where they continue to operate. The final move was not without much controversy among the sea-going fraternity, the added length of sight line causing concern. In recent years the lighting of the buoys has no doubt been of great assistance to mariners.

71. "Blinking Billy" – The Bideford Bar Lighthouse. The High and Low lights in line showed the passage from inside the Bar towards Bideford. The Bar Light, above, was a segmental light showing the white safe passage from the Bar through the channel, and as vessels passed out of this sector it appeared blank or unlit until they entered the red sector after passing the Middle Ridges, warning the vessel to maintain its course towards the two leading lights of the low and high Lights. Known locally as "Blinking Billy" it was sited on the shoreline 1.8 nautical miles south of Saunton cliffs and 1.2 nautical miles north of the High Light. The light was extinguished in 1939, when a minefield approximately 3 miles in length was laid by the British authorities from Saunton Cliffs towards the "Blinking Billy" as a protective measure in wartime. The Light structure was abandoned in September 1946 and subsequently partially demolished down to the roof of the small shelter – Courtesy the late Brian Chugg

72. The remains of "Blinking Billy", erected in 1908 and altered in 1920. The remains of the light were cut up and removed down to the level of the original roof of the small building. By March 2005, when this photo was taken, the level of the sandunes had built up until now the roof was practically level with the sands! –
Courtesy Andrew Byrom.

GROUNDSWELL

The entrances of most North Devon and Cornish harbours were treacherous for sailing vessels except in quiet weather; Bideford Bar is typical of this situation. The reason for this is the persistent groundswell, a feature of this coast, which today provides ideal conditions for young surfers to enjoy their sport.

Any swell at a narrow harbour entrance presents difficulties for vessels, but a groundswell, as it moves into shoal water, develops certain characteristics, which add to these difficulties. The molecules within a wave in deep water merely rise and fall in sequence, which makes the water appear to move along, but the water in fact is stationary. As a wave approaches shallow water there is a tendency for the rising and falling molecules to develop a rotary movement, which eventually has the effect of making the water near the surface actually move with the wave.

The regular regimented waves of a groundswell are particularly prone to this, with the result that such a wave approaching the shore is capable of thrusting floating objects towards the land. As such a wave overtakes a vessel going the same way, the normal flow of water past her rudder is momentarily interrupted and, in effect, she temporarily loses steerage way. The effect of each wave is brief, but it always occurs at the moment when the vessel's tendency to yaw and broach is greatest, with her stern lifted and thrust forward by the swell.

A power-driven vessel approaches a harbour in these conditions with very little 'way' on, so that any tendency to broach can be quickly corrected with a burst of power providing thrust to the rudder. A sailing vessel cannot do this and the practice is to carry plenty of sail and trust to the judgement of the helmsman.

The West Country term to 'take' a harbour is no idle quirk of phraseology but a meaningful description of something, which at times called for considerable experience and skill.

Here in N. Devon when a heavy ground sea is running on the bar the ominous roar it produces carries well inland and often gives cause for comment. In the days of sail with a much smaller population closely bound up with the sea, its significance was profound and a positive talking point.

73. *Braunton Higher Light. The Tide Ball which was raised on a pulley when it was safe to cross the Bar, can be seen to the left of the Lighthouse. The smaller building further to the left was the Low Light, the two lights being about 933ft. (306 metres) apart. The gantry allowed the Low Light to be angled to allow for changing tide and channel conditions. This photo was taken around 1900.   Courtesy R. L. Knight.*

6. WRECK AND RESCUE

David Clement

Wrecks have been noted along this area for many years, perhaps the earliest reported being the loss of two unidentified vessels on the 6 January 1627 when *"Sir John Drake has taken examination and has possession of the goods cast ashore from the wreck,"* and on 23 October 1668 when a vessel laden with tallow and hides from Ireland was wrecked on Braunton Sands. On 25 November 1689 another unidentified vessel was lost on Bideford Bar laden with ammunition and muskets. On 28 November 1735 the *"Johannah & Mary* sailing from Bristol for Africa with tallow, wool and linen was wrecked on Bideford Bar. This was followed by the *"Martha"* on 2 March 1743, homeward bound from the Carolinas, and the *"Amoretta"* on the 5 October 1744 laden with tobacco from Virginia. The ship *"Salisbury"* was the next to be lost on Northam Burrows on 10 March 1749, laden with rum, sugar and general cargo from Jamaica, with only four survivors.

On 23 March 1750 two vessels sailing from Appledore bound for Newfoundland, the *"Pengwin"*, Captain Strange, and the *"Revenge,"* Captain Parlance, both ran aground on the Bar and became total losses. In February 1751 another vessel was lost on the Bar, the *Dieppe Packet"*. This was followed by the *"Union"*, Captain Lockwood, where three crew and three passengers lost their lives; and the *"Charles",* Captain Gegan bound from Bristol for Cork on 25 November 1757. On 8 February 1760 the *"Britannia"* ran ashore on Northam Burrows carrying rum and sugar from New York bound for Bristol, and became a total loss. Near the same position the *"Cwmgwily"*, Captain Sherbon, was a total loss on 2 February 1762 whilst on passage from London to Carmarthen.

There then followed a succession of losses with the following being lost on or about Northam Burrows: the *"Susanna"*, 2 October 1763; the *"Properous"*, Captain Glanville, bound from Neath for Exeter, was embayed and drove ashore on 25 October 1764; the *"Beulah,"* bound from New York, when Captain Green and a number of his crew were drowned was wrecked on 12 November 1764, followed by the *"Three Brothers"* on 21 January 1768 as she crossed the Bar on her way to Bideford. On 17 September 1768 the coal laden *"Seaflower"*, Captain Power, was wrecked.

About the 16 September 1769 the ships *"Sally"*, Captain Barry, laden with lead from Oporto for Bristol, and the *"Three Brothers",* Captain Simpson, also carrying lead ingots were lost on Northam Burrows. Then the *"Juba",* carrying palm oil from Africa, ran ashore on Saunton Sands and was totally lost on 12 December 1770.

Nothing is then reported until the loss of an un-named collier on 25 December 1810 followed by the *"Phoebe"* on 27 September 1811, when her Captain Hardy was drowned. This was followed by the *"Two Patricks"* on 10 March 1812 and *"Scourrier"* 14 October 1812, both of which were lost on the Bar. The Braunton Sands claimed a further victim on 16 January 1816 when the *"Mary & Alicia"* on passage from Cork stranded, and 11 December 1816 saw the loss of the *"Endeavour"*, Captain Bruce, near Northam Burrows. On 18 April 1822 a report was received by the Hydrographic Office advising that the ketch *"Alfred Emma"* had run aground in 1820, northwestward of the Bideford Bar Light and was a total loss. Shifting sands and levels brought the remains of this vessel to the surface again in 2005. In 1821 the *"Bee"* from Fowey struck the Bar and foundered on 2 October, and the following year an unidentified brig went down with the loss of her entire crew on 6 April. Four days later the *"Kitty"*, Captain Widgery, foundered in Bideford Bay with the loss of all except one member of the crew. She was carrying culm from Neath to Bideford. Later the same day another unidentified vessel foundered while crossing the Bar.

And so the list of vessels lost went on. They included the *"Hawke"* and the *"Daniel"* in 1829, the latter on 11 December on the South Tail. This was the first service of the new Appledore Lifeboat *"Volunteer"* which succeeded in rescuing the crew of six and the six passengers aboard. The *"Betsey"* was the next, bound to Barnstaple with coal, also lost crossing the Bar with her crew of three on 3 March 1831. On 20 February 1833 the schooner *"Delabole"* of Truro was wrecked on Saunton Sands, the crew fortunately getting ashore in the ship's boat. The next wreck, the *"Mary Ann"* of Exeter on Northam Burrow on the 24 November 1833, saw the Appledore lifeboat capsized with three of her crew drowned. Three of the brig's crew of four were also lost. On 1 December the *"Sappho"* from Quebec stranded on the Bar and was lost; and seventeen days later the *"Elizabeth"* stranded on Northam Burrows homeward bound from Calcutta. On this occasion the lifeboat provided at Braunton, the *"Assistance"* was launched and took off ten of the crew, the remainder being rescued by the other Appledore boat *"Volunteer"*.

The 22 January 1841 saw the loss of the *"Commerce"* and a year later, on 24 January 1842, the *"Fanny"* entering Bideford from Newport, stranded and went to pieces on the Mixon Sand. The *"Good Intention"* missed stays whilst crossing the Bar and stranded on the North Tail on 26 June 1842. The next vessel to be lost on Northam Burrows was the *"Albert Edward, Prince of Wales"* on 15 January 1843, her crew of 15 being rescued. On the same day another ship, the *"John Lilley"*, went ashore on the Saunton Sands and her remaining crew were also rescued by the same lifeboat which rowed out three times to perform the service. Most of the crew were taken off this vessel before the lifeboat reached her and were landed on the beach inside the Bar. Captain Lamping, the lighthouse keeper who was also the Tide Surveyor, accommodated the 23 crew – mostly drunk – in the lighthouse keeper's cottage.

The next vessel lost on the Bar was the schooner *"Bideford"* which went to pieces as she entered, her crew being saved on 29 February 1848; followed by the *"Dasher"* on the South Tail as she crossed the Bar on 23 March 1850, and the *"Prince Albert"* which drove ashore on the North Tail. On 16 December 1852 the French brig *"Supreme Sagasse"* loaded with coal from Newport was lost with six of her eight crew on the Bar, followed by the *"Torridge"* on 13 September 1853 when she missed stays crossing the Bar in a heavy groundswell. Two more vessels were lost on the Bar in 1854, the *"Marquis"* on 3 January, and the barque *"Secret"* on 18 January which ran aground leaking on North Tail. The *"Henry Patterson"* of Cork grounded on Saunton Sands on 20 October 1854 and became a total loss.

The first RNLI lifeboat to be stationed at Braunton appeared in 1857 and followed the loss of the schooner *"Albion"* of Dartmouth on the North Tail on December 23 1855 when six of the crew of seven were lost. This resulted in a petition from Appledore for an additional lifeboat to be stationed in a more appropriate place to rescue vessels that might come to grief on the Bar. Previous to that a small 26 feet lifeboat, the *"Assistance"* built in 1831, was provided from 1848 by the North Devon Humane Society and the National Shipwreck Institution.

The barque *"Warden"* stranded on Braunton Sands in a hurricane, seven of her eleven crew being drowned, on 8 October 1857. Later in 1857 the *"Dolphin"* a new 28-feet boat was allocated to "Appledore No. 3" station as Braunton was known, by the RNLI, which proved its usefulness by going to the assistance of the schooner *"Revenge"* of Falmouth on May 29, 1858. The schooner had driven ashore on the North Tail whilst bound from Dublin for Cardiff. The master was brought ashore to arrange for assistance to get his vessel off and the story ended satisfactorily as the vessel was salvaged little damaged. The brig *"North Esk"* of Sunderland was the next major service during hurricane conditions on November 2 1859, when *Dolphin* saved the six crew, again from the North Tail, shortly before the vessel went to pieces. Her last recorded service on January 1 1863 was to the ship *"Louisa"* of Bristol, when she was able to rescue 20 persons. This vessel, owned by the local shipowner William Yeo, was on passage from Venice to Cardiff in ballast and became embayed in Bideford Bay. Two tugs attempted to tow her to safety but following the loss of the tow ropes she was driven onto Saunton Sands from where the crew were rescued. Perhaps surprisingly she was later salvaged and repaired and continued to trade into the early 1900s. The *Dolphin's* last recorded service, albeit unsuccessful, was to the schooner "*Meridian*" of Fowey on 15 November 1864, which owing to the weather conditions she was unable to reach. The vessel went ashore on Saunton Sands and at low tide the crew were able to reach shore themselves with difficulty. Captain Lamping, the lighthouse keeper noticed the wreck and went to Saunton Court to raise the alarm and to arrange for the lifeboat to be launched. The "*Meridian*" had been built in 1822 at Torquay.

In the meantime the schooner *"Clifton"* of Gloucester was lost on the Bar on 12 March 1858, the *"Ellen Gwenllian"* on 26 October 1859, with the schooner *"Swan"* bound to Cardiff with copper ore on the same date. No less than twelve sailing vessels were wrecked in the vicinity on this day, many in Morte Bay. 1859 was a dreadful year as the schooner *"Refuge"* grounded with the loss of her entire crew with the barque *"Wanderer"* grounding near the wreck of the *"North Esk"* on 1 November 1859 and again losing her entire crew of eleven. On the same day the sloop *Peace"* was also lost on Bideford Bar. The next loss on the Bar was the schooner *"David & Martha"* laden with coal, which stranded on the South Tail.

In April 1866 a new 32-foot lifeboat, the *"George & Catherine"*, named after the benefactors Mr & Mrs George Jeremy of Axminster, arrived on the station, which by then had become the independent station of Braunton, although the crew of the lifeboat still came from Appledore – a practice that continued until the end of the station. This was a self-righting boat having a crew of ten oarsmen and up to 3 supernumeraries. She remained on the station until 1881.

On 21 September 1866 the ketch *"Wool Packet"* of Dartmouth drove ashore on the Bar. Thinking she could be got off a number of men from Appledore went aboard but the weather deteriorated, resulting in the pilot gig *"Volunteer"* going alongside and taking off four men. The tug *"Ely"* from Cardiff was in the river Taw and being piloted by the lifeboat coxswain, managed to take off the remaining nine men before the vessel went to pieces. Although the Braunton lifeboat was not launched on that occasion the coxswain, James Smallridge, was awarded an RNLI medal for bravery, as was the master of the tug, Captain Thomas Jones.

1867 saw the loss of the smack *"Mary"* on 5 January and the French schooner *"Jeune Adeline"* from St. Malo on 1 December, the latter fortunately without loss of men.
The *"George & Catherine"* was responsible for assisting the brig *"Ruth"* of London, which drove ashore on Saunton Sands, when she rescued her crew of nine on 17 October 1867. Her next service was assisting the Appledore lifeboat going to the assistance of two sailing vessels embayed in Bideford Bay on December 28, 1868 when the Austrian barque *"Pace"* ran ashore on Northam Sands. The Appledore lifeboat rescued eight crew, four more being drowned, the remaining nine crew walking ashore at low tide.

The next vessel to be lost on the Bar was the Penzance schooner *"Pride of the West"* on 3 May 1869, followed by the schooner *"Reliance"* on 12 September 1869 with the loss of her crew of four. She was bound from Swansea to Fremington with coal.

The next lifeboat service in a heavy southwesterly gale was to the brigantine *"Nigretta"* from New York on November 15, 1871, which drove ashore, when the *George and Catherine* saved seven crew, including the 2nd Mate who had previously been washed overboard. On 21 December 1871 the schooner *"Brothers"* of Milford Haven was lost on Northam Sands. Then 10 October 1873 saw the loss of the schooner *"Tulip"* laden with salt from Gloucester, which stranded on Saunton Sands and broke up. Of her crew of five, three men were lost.

The last recorded service of this lifeboat was to the schooner *"Caroline"* when five passengers were rescued on 31 August 1874. She was a regular packet bound to Bideford from Swansea when, crossing the bar, her fore topmast carried away and she ran aground on the North Tail. Her passengers were landed and she was later salvaged and continued trading until 1913. Interestingly she had previously been the subject of a rescue on 11 March 1859 when the Northam lifeboat rescued five crew when she was driven ashore whilst on passage from Teignmouth to Newport and became embayed. She was subsequently salvaged.

The coxswain of the Braunton lifeboat, James Harvey, was involved in two rescues subsequently, although the lifeboat was not launched. On 13 February 1875 the deeply laden limestone carrier *"Lydney Trader"* ran aground on the Bar as she attempted to enter in light winds, and afterwards went to pieces in the heavy groundswell shortly after the crew were taken off.

The next vessel to be lost, on 20 February 1877 was the *"Muse"*, a French brigantine carrying pitch from Gloucester for St. Nazaire, which became embayed in Barnstaple Bay and ran aground on Saunton Sands with the loss of four of her five crew. The *"Muse"* was off Lundy Island when the weather deteriorated and the master turned back intending to put into Cardiff. The vessel found herself embayed in Bideford Bay in a northwesterly gale and struck on Saunton sands. She had broken up within three hours. The Braunton lifeboat was not launched as the disaster had occurred before anyone ashore had realised the situation.

She was followed by the schooner *"Heroine"* on 24 March 1878 bringing a cargo of coal to Barnstaple from Lydney, which stranded on the Bar. Later the *"Ann"* bringing coal to Bideford was stranded near the Braunton Lighthouse on 3 August and went to pieces.

On July 20 1879 the *"Three Brothers"* left the Taw Estuary bound for Newport but was dismasted shortly after crossing the bar. The crew took to their boat and made fast to the Fairway Buoy, but their plight was not realised by those ashore until it was too late. The Braunton lifeboat was launched but by the time they reached the Fairway Buoy the crew had been lost. The *"Three Brothers"* afterwards drove ashore and was broken up.

In August 1881 a new 34-foot lifeboat arrived, the *"Robert & Catherine"*, which was named in memory of a Miss Leicester's parents who lived in Bayswater, London. Built at a cost of £363 she remained on station until 1902.

With the improved guidance into the estuary the numbers of vessels coming to grief reduced. It was not until 1884 that the next vessels stranded, the first being the brigantine *"Jonathan Weir"* on 23 January which was disabled in heavy weather and drifted ashore near Down End, fortunately without loss of her crew. On 7 December 1884 another brigantine, the *"Chalciope"* of Fleetwood, ran aground on Saunton Sands and went to pieces. She had grounded in a thick fog and a west-southwesterly gale one mile from Downend on the northern edge of the Sands. The Braunton lifeboat took off three injured crew members. 1885 saw the loss of the schooner *"Ellen Dawson"* on 9 September, which stranded on the Bar and became a total loss. On 25 September 1886 the schooner *"Strathisla"* attempted to enter the estuary in a fog but ran ashore on the North Ridge and broke up off Millstone Point. This was followed by the schooner *"Superior"* of Fowey, which had left Fremington with a cargo of china clay and struck on the bar as she left the estuary and foundered on 26 October 1886; followed by the schooner *"Saint Louis"*, which stranded on Saunton Sands on 12 December and became a total loss.

The next losses were on the 8/9 January 1888, when the ketch *"Boscoppa"* of Padstow bringing coal to Fremington, and the the schooner *"Atlanta"* of Bideford also carrying coal inwards, both came to grief on the Bar and went to pieces. Wind conditions were comparatively calm, but the groundswell had built up huge seas. In similar conditions the ketch *"Ruby"* of Bideford was lost on the Bar on 9 August. 1899 saw the loss of the sloop *"Charlotte Ann"* of Fowey, again bringing coal to Fremington.

The next major rescue was that of the iron ship *"Penthesilea"* of Liverpool on 20 January 1890 bound from Newport for Mauritius with coal under Captain Frederick Wilson. It is interesting to look at this unusually successful event through the pages of *Lloyd's List* which shows the vessel left Newport with coal, bound for Mauritius on 9 January 1890. Bad weather seems to have been encountered from the start as a week later on 16 January it was reported that the *Penthesilea* was spoken 10 miles north-west of Lundy, 80 miles from Newport. She subsequently ran ashore on 20 January. Launched soon after high water the Braunton lifeboat took fourteen survivors on board and landed these by means of a chain gang of individuals standing in the surf to carry them to safety, before the putting back to the wreck where she rescued the remaining seventeen crew.

Lloyd's List then published a number of reports:

74. The iron ship "Penthesilea" of Liverpool, lying at Fowey. She was wrecked on North Tail, Braunton January 1890 carrying coal. Her crew of 31 were rescued by the Braunton lifeboat "Robert & Catherine" (I). The ship was afterwards salvaged and continued in trade until the early 1900s. – David Clement Collection.

20, January – Braunton, 9.09am. "Penthesilea" ship, Newport for Mauritius, coal laden, ashore Saunton Sands. Crew saved.

Liverpool 20 January, 3.22pm Following telegram received by owners states: "Penthesilea" ashore Saunton Sand, decks swept clean, vessel full of water, don't think at present any chance of getting ship off. Sandy bottom.

London 21 January. The Liverpool Salvage Association reports under date Liverpool 21 January, 10.32am as follows: "Penthesilea" lies end-on the sands about one mile south of Baggy Point.

Liverpool 21 January, 6.53pm. Liverpool Salvage Association reports: "Penthesilea" dries half tide, stern out embedded five feet, slight list, bilge butts and "landing" leaking badly, other butts strained, keel broken and large hole there aft, rudder gone, mainmast up two inches, part port bulwarks gone, deck houses gutted. Engaged sending down hamper and arranging to run out spare anchor. Other anchors lost. At this time they were busy sending down her masts, yards and rigging.

London, 21 January: The salvage association had received the following telegram from Captain Gillon, dated Braunton 21 January: "Penthesilea" stranded three miles North and East from Braunton Lighthouse, head to land, dry at half tide, rudder gone, sternpost and keel twisted to starboard, starboard bilge landing and butts started, water falls in hold through bottom, mainmast set up, deck houses gutted, both anchors with part cable gone. Now dismantling top gear, probably to lower masthead. Part cargo must be disposed of. Will report further as to prospects.

Liverpool 22 January, 6.48pm. Liverpool Salvage Association reports "Penthesilea", More damage to poop houses by last night's gale, little more list, but otherwise position unchanged.

Liverpool 27 January, 12.05pm. Following telegram received this morning from Braunton: 9.55am "Penthesilea" heavy gale last night and yesterday. More settled today. No alteration.

Liverpool 30 January 12.29pm. Liverpool Salvage Association reports "Penthesilea" Discharging commenced onto beach. Weather finer, but tides scarcely leave the vessel. Fear may not be ready by next springs unless quantity of cargo is jettisoned.

Liverpool 18 February, 6.03pm. Liverpool Salvage Association report that "Penthesilea" was floated this afternoon.

Bideford, 19 February 11.22am. "Penthesilea" was safely towed into Appledore last evening.

After being taken to the dry dock at Appledore, the *Penthesilea* returned to Liverpool on 24 May, and following completion of repairs, sailed for San Francisco on 20 October 1890. She continued to trade until the early 1900s.

75. Braunton lifeboat photographed around 1890 – Braunton Museum

76. The occasion in 1902 when Braunton took delivery of its new lifeboat – the second "Robert & Catherine", with the ten-horse team that launched and recovered the boat and – on the right the coxswain, his deputy and the number "3" with the crew. The crew consisted of 13 men but in this photograph the reserves are also shown with them. On the far right is the lifeboat house. – Courtesy Robert Andrew.

The next wreck occurred on 30 June 1890 when the ketch *"Industry"* of Bridgwater was lost on Braunton Sands whilst bound out for Lydney, followed a month later by the local ketch *"Elizabeth"* bound for Appledore with limestone on 7 July. On 18 December the fishing smack *"Gem"* from Bideford foundered following a collision with the ketch *"Fame."*

There were then no further losses until on 4 July 1892 the ketch *"Ellen Williams"* of Bidoford stranded on the North Tail after becoming embayed in the Bay. 1894 saw the *"Roe"*, another Bideford ketch wrecked by the groundswell breaking on the Bar in light

77. The wreck of the "Phyllis Grey" thrown on Saunton Sands 9 September 1908.

78. Braunton Life Boat house in the early 1900s with the lifeboat "Robert & Catherine" ready for service. The lifeboat house was removed when the station closed in 1918, being dismantled soon after, having been sold for £25.

wind conditions, whilst attempting to enter from Lydney with coal. She was followed by the ketch *"Charlotte"* of Chester, bringing coal to Barnstaple on the 2 October 1895. Another local fishing smack, the *"Kate"* was lost on 5 November, followed by the *"Active"* on 19 May 1896, which had sailed from Clovelly with fish for Bideford. *"Carrick"* a brigantine from Dundalk, was the next loss on 6 December, which was proceeding to Cardiff to load coal. She stranded on Northam Burrows and went to pieces.

The Braunton lifeboat went to the assistance of the ketch *"John"* of Barnstaple on 2 March 1897, which was bringing coal to Bideford and went ashore on a shoal near the Bar Buoy. She was followed by the *"Joseph & Thomas"* of Bideford on 7 April 1899, the vessel foundering off Down End Point with the loss of two of her crew of three. In July 1902 the Braunton lifeboat was replaced with the *"Robert & Catherine" (II)*, a 34ft. vessel rowing ten oars. She was not called upon to perform any services during her presence at the station, but did capsize on 21 December 1911, fortunately without loss of life. At this time there were three lifeboats on the estuary.

On 14 December 1902 the smack *"Pioneer"* of Bideford came to grief on the estuary Bar. The following year in September 1903, the brigantine *"Flimby"* was lost on the Bar on the 11th, her five crew being rescued by the Appledore lifeboat. In 1904 the regular strandings continued with the loss of the ketch *"Cornucopia"* inward bound with coal for Fremington on the 8 July 1904, followed a month later on 6 August by the *"Salome"* which was wrecked inward bound from Clovelly with the loss of her crew of two. The 14 January 1905 saw the loss of the ketch *"Advance"* of Bideford again on the Bar.

As engines began to be fitted to sailing vessels the rate of losses reduced, the next being the ketch *"Model"* which stranded on 13th March 1911 outward bound from Appledore for Lydney to load coal. She was followed by the ketch *"Comet"* inward bound for Barnstaple with coal on 8 January 1913.

79. Braunton Lifeboat *"Robert & Catherine"* launching. The vessel was manned by men from Appledore, bringing their smaller boat to Crow Point and walking to the lifeboat house. Braunton men were responsible for launching the boat and supplying the horses. – Braunton Museum

80. Recovering the lifeboat – Braunton Museum

The third *"Robert & Catherine"* lifeboat had arrived at Braunton in May 1912. Perhaps her best-known feat was the rescue of the crew of four from the schooner *"Old Head"* of Cork on 19 July 1917, which struck the North Tail in a heavy ground swell and later rolled over several times before going to pieces. The new lifeboat had been built at a cost of £953 by the Thames Ironworks at Blackwall. On 4 October 1917 the *"Surprise"* a schooner laden with coal was lost on the Bar with two of her five crew. The 23 March 1918 saw the loss of the schooner *"Volant"* of Belfast on Braunton Sands. By 1918 most of those responsible for launching the lifeboat, together with the horses used, had been called up for War Service, and the Braunton lifeboat station was closed. Initially this was on a temporary basis, but in 1919 the lifeboat house was sold for £25 and dismantled.

In 1922 the elderly *Alfred & Emma* owned in Braunton, stranded on Saunton Sands and went to pieces.

The next and last significant wreck in the area was the loss of the ketch *"Ceres"* of Bude, the oldest vessel on the British Register at the time having been built in 1811. She had left Swansea with basic slag bound for Bude and sprang an uncontrollable leak, foundering off Baggy Point 24 November 1936.

Since that time there have been few incidents to disturb the local community. The first was the loss of the motor fishing vessel *"Rossekop II"* on 4 November 1972 which drove ashore on Bideford Bar. On 8 October 1976 the fishing vessel *"Diane"* capsized on the Bar and later broke up whilst attempting to enter the estuary in rough weather.

It can be seen how dangerous the entrance to this estuary was during the days of sail. At least six other vessels, so far unidentified, are known to have been lost in this area. The details of vessels above show principally those that were totally lost. Many more ran aground in less straitened circumstances and were successfully got off, but the reason why this estuary needed no less than three lifeboats must be very apparent. Apart from the lifeboats to rescue persons after the event, the marking of the entrance was of prime importance, which was discussed in the preceding chapter.

Wreck and rescue did not only occur on the Bar as the Bristol Channel with its very great rise and fall of tide (it is the second highest range of tide in the World) was a dangerous waterway. Some incidents however occurred close to home, as can be seen with the *"Dido C"*, illustrated in the Alphabetical Schedule of vessels, (page 153) which was fortunate to get off the rocks she went aground on.

On 29 May 1929 the ketch *"Lewisman"* was responsible for saving the lives of the crew of the ketch *"F.A.M.E."*. Capt. Frank Mitchell and his mate and brother, John Mitchell, of the *"Lewisman"*, both of Braunton, were presented with purses in recognition of their bravery in saving the captain and mate of the sailing vessel *"F.A.M.E."*, also of Braunton, the presentation being made by Mr. H. C. Whitehead, of Bideford, the hon. Secretary of the Appledore Branch of the Royal National Lifeboat Institution. On 29 May 1929 the two vessels left Braunton, bound for Ilfracombe. The sailing auxiliary *"Lewisman"* towed the *"F.A.M.E."* over the bar and then went ahead. When out at sea the two vessels encountered a gale near Bull Point. The force of the storm was such that without warning, the *"F.A.M.E."* found her mast carried away and with it a good deal of her deck. The vessel rapidly foundered, and Captain. William Tucker and his mate, Reginald Williams, took to their boat in the nick of time. Meantime the *"Lewisman"* had gained on her by about 3½ miles, and had reached the shelter of Lee harbour. She observed the *"F.A.M.E.'s"* plight, however, and put back into the gale to her assistance. This took some time, during which the two men from the *"F.A.M.E."* expected every moment to be their last, as their small boat was rapidly filling, and in danger of being swamped at any minute. By the efforts of the two Mitchell brothers however, they were finally rescued, but not before the boat was twice lost to sight and hope given up.

81. The topsail schooner "Volant" ashore on Saunton Sands, Easter Thursday 1917
Braunton Museum

82. An unknown wreck uncovered on Saunton Sands – February 2005
Andrew Byrom

7. THE MARINERS OF BRAUNTON

The late Stan Rogers and David Clement

About 1850, there was a big export of cattle to America. Those who had helped to breed the animals followed in their hundreds. In April 1851 thirty people left Braunton to start a new life in America. Some members of Braunton families I remember were Gould, Johnson and Luscombe who emigrated in the early 1900's.

Many local men manned the ships concerned, some of these ships were built at Barnstaple, Bideford and Appledore. Probably the largest built at Barnstaple was the "*Lady Ebrington*". The builders were Westacotts who had a shipyard on the south bank opposite Castle Quay. She was a full rigged ship and her captain was a Braunton man named Gammon. The owners were the "North Devon Shipping Co". During the Australian gold rush in the 1850's she carried many men and their families who expected to make their fortunes in that land. The *"Lady Ebrington"* made several trips as an "emigrant" ship and was eventually lost at sea on a voyage from America to this country. The crew of fourteen were never heard of. Many of these old sailing ships just disappeared. The dangers that faced these emigrants were tremendous.

One incident will serve as a reminder. The barque "*John*" of Plymouth sailed on a fine evening in May for Quebec under the command of Captain E. Rawle. On board were 240 Devonian and Cornish emigrants bound for Canada. Only a few hours later their voyage came to an abrupt end. At Molland near the church doorway there is a memorial stone telling a sad story.

> *"Erected to the memory and to record the disastrous death of Thomas and Sarah Pincombe of this parish and their youthful family of six sons and daughters all of whom perished by shipwreck together with 187 of their fellow passengers".*

This tragic event happened on the Manacle Rocks near Helford, Cornwall on the night of 3 May 1855, just six hours after leaving Plymouth. The "*John*" was 45 years old when she foundered. She was sent to sea without a signal gun or distress rockets of any sort and was carrying twice as many passengers as she was built for. At the inquest the jury returned a verdict of manslaughter against Captain Rawle.

Coming nearer home, in the early 1900's many folk were carried in local ships to South Wales to work in the coalmines and steel works. There were constant crossings of relatives to see these new wonders. "Emigrants" returning for holidays told of their new found prosperity. Many made a habit of coming home for Barnstaple Fair. In addition to passengers all kinds of freight was carried. Iron and copper ore were loaded at Combe Martin, Watermouth and Velator. There is a small quantity of iron ore still left by the quay at Velator. This came from the mines at Spreacombe. During the summer months there was a considerable trade for small craft carrying limestone and coal from South

Wales to various beaches on the North Devon coast. Lime burning was a big industry. There were three kilns at Velator, six at various places on Barnstaple river, and others at Croyde, Putsborough and Woolacombe.

Cargoes of barley and pit props and smaller amounts of tin plate boxes, potatoes, carrots and mangolds were loaded at Velator. The two latter items were for the pit ponies in South Wales. The "Harriett" took the last cargo of carrots from Fremington. Another vessel, the "*Comet*" took some part cargoes of pottery for Fishleys of Fremington. With the coming of the railway, Fremington became a very busy place. Thousands of tons of coal were discharged there as well as timber and basic slag. Many cargoes of clay from the Marland area were loaded from the quays. Part of the original railway bridge was made to open and small vessels were able to pass through to discharge their cargoes in the "Pill". Then there was gravel. Hundreds of cargoes were taken from Crow to help build the docks at Swansea, Barry, Cardiff, Bristol, Newport and Avonmouth. This gravel was also used to build the foundations of the Transporter Bridge at Newport. Cargoes were taken to all the small ports from Ilfracombe to Gloucester. With the coming of "sand-suckers" this trade died out.

Cargoes brought back to Braunton and Barnstaple were coal, salt, manure, basic slag, grain, flour, timber, bricks, tiles, pipes, cement, slates and cracked stones. The following are interesting items connected with Barnstaple. From the *North Devon Journal,* May 1854. "Return of bells to Pilton. The ship "*John and Ann*" arrived at Barnstaple on the 11th having as part of her cargo, five bells, three re-cast and two new for the tower of Pilton Church, thus increasing the peal to eight".

South Molton Town Hall is part of a mansion erected at Morwenstow, North Cornwall. It was demolished, brought by sea to Barnstaple and then by road to South Molton. Horses and carts and packhorses were used. The cost of the section of the mansion bought for South Molton was £178. Shipment by sea, packhorse charges, labour for re-erecting and materials used cost altogether £1,000.

For some time, a schooner, the "*Waterwitch*" owned by local businessmen ran from Bristol to Bideford with general cargo. Later on a small steamer, the "*Devonia*", carried on this trading until it was killed by road transport.

Velator was a playground for many youngsters from Braunton and among other things model yacht sailing was very popular. At this time the river was clean and people were baptized there and also at Wrafton above the bridge. When the local council decided to empty the sewerage into the river that put paid to swimming and paddling. For years some of us fought the Parish Council but they could not, or would not see anything wrong and for a long time the river was like an open sewer. Eventually the present treatment works were built.

Velator was once a busy place especially on spring tides. At times there were three vessels discharging coal for various merchants. This was often retailed direct from the ship. Horses and carts and butts were used. It took two or three days to discharge, according to the number of horses available. Many farmers from the district fetched their own coal. 'The price before 1914 was around £1 per ton.

Freights were low. Vessels were paid 3/6d to 4/- (£0.17p. to £020p.) per ton for gravel out of which 8d went to the Parish Council and Trinity House. Coal from Ely Harbour to Fremington 2/9 to 3/- (£0.13p. to £0.15p.) per ton. Newport to Braunton or Barnstaple 4/-. (£0.20p.) and from Lydney 4/6. (£0.22p) per ton. Bricks from Bridgwater were carried at an agreed price per 1,000. Freights rose during the 1914-18 war but slumped afterwards.

In addition to the vessels there were barges bringing gravel from the river. At certain times of the year there was a big trade in seaweed. This was used as manure by farmers and gardeners. Special boats were used for this trade. Some Appledore boats came loaded with seaweed and took back potatoes. Among the names of Braunton men engaged in this work were Crick, Bassett, Phillips, Parkin, Paddison, Mitchell, Mullen and Quick.

There were two ship-repairing yards at Velator. The first was on Wrafton bank and was owned and worked by Mr Fred Clarke. Sometime after that closed down another yard on the opposite bank was opened by Messrs W. Bray and E. Evans. They were very busy for some years fitting auxiliary engines into local vessels and doing general repairs. Their workshop is now a waste paper store. The whole area is now taken over by pleasure craft of all shapes and sizes. In the old days the vessels created a great deal of work for W. Braund and Sons, sailmakers who had a loft in South Street.

The finest vessel to come to Velator was the three masted schooner "*Katie*" of Bideford, built by Cox of Appledore. She brought a cargo of manure for Mr Charles Symonds of Church Street. A gig and crew from Appledore towed her up the Pill one fine morning.

At the outbreak of the 1914-18 war there were probably 150 vessels belonging to Braunton and Appledore. They were mainly sailing craft. I remember being one of over 60 going out on one tide. Old men said that they could remember 100 going out. It required great skill to keep them from colliding in a narrow channel over the bar.

There was great competition to get to the port of discharge first. The time taken varied according to the wind and capabilities of the various vessels. Of course there was great rivalry between the crews. With a good fair wind we would get to Swansea, Barry, Cardiff or Newport on the same day. If there was a head wind or no wind at all it was a different story. The vessels varied in size from about 230 tons down to 45 tons. They were three and two masted schooners and ketches mostly engaged in the coasting trade. Cargoes were taken to various ports in the British Isles. There was a big trade to Ireland, Channel Islands and ports on the continent. Some of the larger vessels went to Spain, Portugal and Iceland. The smaller ketches traded mostly in the Bristol Channel. Coal was taken to places in South Wales like Tenby, Caldy Island, Saundersfoot, Solva and St. Davids. Some went on to load cracked roadstone at Porthgain for Barnstaple R.D.C. and Braunton Quay.

During the summer months many traded to places on the Cornish coast like Bude, Padstow, Wadebridge, Newquay and St. Ives. Ports on the south coast of Cornwall were commonly known as "being round the land". Places like Cadgwith, Falmouth, Truro, Helford and others came under this heading.

Many of the vessels were owned by the men who sailed them. The masters were given the name of "captain" but they had no real standing. However, there were some who passed examinations and commanded large ships. Among these were Bert and Bill Elliott, Jack Reed, Alfred Heath and Donald Pugsley. The two latter had charge of large sailing ships trading all over the world.

One very interesting character who was for some time in old sailing ships was Richard Mullen of Velator. He used to tell me of how he ran away to sea when he was about 15, and eventually signed on aboard a sailing ship bound for New York. He went ashore and was "shanghaied" and the next thing he knew he was on another sailing ship bound round Cape Horn. It took a long time as they met bad weather. Eventually they reached one of the ports on the west coast of South America. Conditions were so bad on the voyage that Richard and his mate decided to run away once they got on shore. They went inland for some miles where they met a man on a mule and made him understand that they wanted work. He got them jobs in a mine. This was a very hard life but they stuck it until such time as they reckoned that the ship had sailed. Then they went back to the coast and signed on aboard another ship and worked their way back to this country. Quite an exciting venture for two young men.

Coming back to Braunton. Locally a trip began at the port of discharge. It was a common sight to see men walking to Barnstaple in the early morning to reach their vessels. When empty, if there was wind they sailed down the river but if it was calm the vessels were often towed along by the crew of the boat. This was sometimes followed when the vessels were loaded. Some vessels carried "sweeps", long oars, and these were also used in calm weather. Other methods were "warping" and "tracking".

Warping was usually carried out with two men in the boat. A kedge - a small anchor - carried in the stern with rope attached was pulled away until the order given by the pilot "heave out". The kedge was then thrown overboard, care being taken to see that it was the right way up. Attached to the crown was a buoy rope with a piece of wood or a bunch of corks on the end. This was held by one of the men while the other worked both oars to keep the boat straight ready for the next move. The rope was taken to the hand winch aboard the vessel and wound in. When the distance between the vessel and boat was short, the order "weigh away" was given. The kedge was pulled up and the process repeated. The length of warp used varied according to the turns in the channel. In the "*Acacia*" we had a pair of paddles and on occasions when short of help, warping was carried out with one man in the boat. In this event the kedge was carried in the bow. This generally meant that the boat was facing in the right direction for the next move. In both cases speed and skill were necessary.

Tracking was carried out by men on the riverbank pulling the vessel along by a rope. Amongst the places where this happened was along the cutting from Velator Quay to the Toll House, from Barnstaple Railway Bridge through the Drawbridge to Pilton, and on the canal at Lydney.

Payment in those days was by the trip - the same sum whether it took three days, three weeks or even longer. As a rule, gravel was the outward cargo but if there was no demand for this, a few tons of sand were thrown in as ballast. In some cases this was taken out free depending on the place of loading. At other times it had to be thrown overboard. There was no pay for master or crew in either case.

It was considered part of the job. The duration of the trip depended mainly on wind and weather.

Life was not easy in those days. During the winter there were long periods when vessels were windbound and sailors and their families found life very hard. The position of wives were especially so. It was marvellous how they managed. They made great sacrifices for their children. It was always a case of "putting by" during the summer for winter days. There was no unemployment pay or social security in the old days and sailors turned their hands to all sorts of odd jobs, especially on farms when they could not go to sea. Many belonged to "friendly" societies like the "Oddfellows" and "National Deposit" so as to get some small benefit in case of sickness.

By the end of 1914-18 war it was plain that small sailing coasters were doomed. Freights became more difficult to obtain. There was great competition from the railways and later road transport. Gradually the numbers decreased and vessels were sold and used for other purposes. Winter gales took their toll and some were lost often with all the crew. Vessels which had carried a crew of three now sailed with two and found it hard to make a living. The advent of oil engines kept some going for a number of years but they gradually disappeared. The "*Bessie Clarke*" was the first Braunton ketch to have an engine installed. Today there is not a single coaster left in Braunton and Appledore. The last to leave was the schooner "*Result*". She is now a museum ship in Ireland where she was built. The last remaining, "*Kathleen and May*" of Appledore, restored by Steve Clarke is now at Bideford, but even her future is uncertain.

I have said that life was hard at times but there were compensations. A great deal of fun was to be had and numerous jokes were played on each other. One tends to forget the worst parts and remember the better. The glorious sunrises and sunsets, the smell of burning gorse coming off the land on a summer evening, the wonder of seeing the reflections of the aurora borealis, the beauty of a clear night when the stars seemed to hang in the sky, the thrilling sight of a lunar rainbow seen at 3.am one stormy night when anchored off Stead Island at the mouth of Bridgwater River. These and many other similar happenings bring back lovely memories for me. Then there was the great feeling of fellowship which exists among seamen. It was always instilled into me that if anyone needed help it was, if at all possible, to be given freely and willingly.

THE BRAUNTON MARITIME FAMILIES

The community around Braunton and the associated villages of Wrafton and Velator saw specific families connected with the sea and shipping interests generally, often for many generations. Whilst Braunton was principally an agrarian community, families maintained interests in both.

Some of the well-known families involved in seafaring were:

Ayres	Dendle	Lane	Redmore
	Daniel	Lamey	Reed
Bassett	Drake	Lamprey	Rook
Baglole	Dunn	Lynch	Rogers
Braund		Luscombe	Roulstone
Bray	Elliott		

Butler		Manley	Scobling
Bidder	Gould	Mitchell	Slee
		Mullen	Stevens
Clarke	Hancock		Stribbling
Coats	Hartnoll	Newcombe	
Chugg	Harris		Thompson
Comber	Heath	Packwood	Tucker
Chichester	Herniman	Paddison	
Coles	Hunt	Parkhouse	Watts
Cottle	Huxtable	Parkin	Welch
Corney		Passmore	Westacott
Crick	Incledon	Phillips	White
Cook	Irwin	Pugsley	Williams

We meet many of these families as we pass through this book and the schedule of Braunton vessels that follows, but here are just a few of the later mariners during the transition from sail.

Captain George Chugg was born in 1841 at Wrafton, died aged 90 years in 1931. He obtained his Masters Certificate by examination at Barnstaple on 19 December 1868, at the age of 27 as seen below, and went on to command and own various Braunton based sailing vessels, followed by his son, also George, who commanded the *"Waterlily"*. With his brothers and sons, some five generations of the Chugg family were at sea.

83. Certificate of Competency – Captain George Chugg, 1868 – Braunton Museum

Another well-known Braunton family were the Clarkes who both sailed and owned many vessels, and inter-married with other families having similar interests – the Mitchells and the Corneys for example. Whilst the sea life was clearly hard, most lived to a good age.

84. Thomas Clarke, John Mitchell and John Clarke – three ninety-year-old ex-masters of Braunton sailing vessels seen in 1934. – Courtesy Sam Mitchell

The Mitchell family in particular were amongst the last of the families regularly engaged in the sailing trades, from running coasters in the short sea coastwise trades, to loading gravel in their barge *"Hilda"*, the last sailing barge in trade. We are particularly indebted to Bill and Sam Mitchell for making available their collection of evocative photographs for this book. Similarly to other families one generation followed the next in gaining employment from the sea. The auxiliary ketch *"Lewisman"* was still trading to the mid-1940s with Captain Frank Mitchell and his brother John as mate. Bill Mitchell sailed with his father aboard the *"Agnes"* when aged just six. Leaving school aged 14 in 1942 he joined full-time as cook. In 1944 he became mate and following his fathers retirement, the skipper in 1952. As cargoes fell away the vessel became uneconomic and was sold to Captain Peter Herbert of Bude in 1955.

85. Three generations William, Samuel and Frank Mitchell courtesy Sam Mitchell

86. Fred Mitchell, Tom Welch, Frank Mitchell and an unknown member of the crew of *"Result"* – courtesy Sam Mitchell

Another Mitchell, Sam, is still with us. He went to sea aged 14 years with his father in the *"Traly"* and later in the *"Result"* until 1955/6, before working on the gravel barge *"JJRP"* with his uncle Fred Mitchell. His memories are of the sheer hard work involved in discharging cargoes of roadstone, coal and basic slag, and the manner in which road transport captured those trades in which these vessels operated, until cargoes became scarce. Work on the gravel barges was equally hard.

Bill Mitchell, who has been previously mentioned has been of tremendous help in the compiling of this book with his collection of photographs and memorabilia

87. Sam Mitchell   *88. Bill Mitchell*

Thomas Clarke Welch, later to own the *"Result"*, sailed deep-water, joining firstly the barque *"Miefield"* and leaving Liverpool 18 August 1906 bound for Corral, Valparaiso and Antofagasta, Chile. As this was a typical round voyage of the period we give the details. Arriving at Corral on 20 December after a passage of 124 days they discharged their cargo and loaded beer and timber for Antofagasta. Leaving Corral under tow with the help of a steam whaler on 23 January 1907 they anchored in Valparaiso 28 January, and discharged further cargo before leaving 9 March for Antofagasta, where they arrived on the 15 March. After discharging the remainder of the cargo from Liverpool, together with the beer and timber loaded earlier, they left in ballast for Ilo Ilo on 26 April. Arriving 4 May, they received orders and departed 8 May for a number of small Peruvian ports where they loaded guano. After loading stores in Callao in August they proceeded to Santa Island to complete loading, arriving on 12th August, and left 5 September with a full cargo of guano bound for Glasgow, where they arrived Saturday 3 January 1908. Captain William Drummond wrote that he had *found him strictly sober, smart and attentive to his duties. I wish him every success in his future career.* This was an unusual expression for a ship's master to use.

Tom Welch then joined the *"Castleton"*, built in Port Glasgow in 1903, under Captain John Roberts. He was a seaman aboard from 17 June 1908 until 24 April 1909. Of just 1,971 tons gross she was the average size of sailing vessel at that time. Captain Roberts also wrote glowingly that *I found him steady and attentive to each and all of his duties. I can highly recommend him to anyone who may require his services.*

89. *The 3-,masted ship "Castleton" David Clement Collection*

Thereafter he sat and passed his examination in Cardiff for Second Mate on 7 July 1909 and later as a fully qualified master, returned to the coasting trade and Braunton.

His son, Peter Welch became owner in turn of the *"Result"*, and his grandson, also Tom Welch has written of the *Result* in this book. He joined the Bank Line at the start of his career. His other grandson, Peter also sailed on the *"Result"* for a period.

90. The barque "Claverdon" in which John Elliott served.

Herbert J. (John) Elliot, born in 1892, to John Elliott, the local Braunton blacksmith, first went to sea aged 15½ in a coastal schooner and then joined the 3-masted barque *"Claverdon"* sailing in November 1908 to the West coast of South America and paying off in Hamburg where she had taken nitrates, in December 1909. His sister, Marigold, married into another Braunton seafaring family – Captain John Clarke, owner of the *"Traly"* and the *"Democrat."* John Elliott later joined Houlders Steamship Line *"Oldfield Grange"* as Third Officer in June 1913 and ended his career as Houlder's Bristol Channel Cargo Superintendent, retiring in September 1958.

Captain William Howard Elliott was born in Braunton 23 December 1900, and joined Alfred Holt & Co, gaining his Master's Certificate in 1928. Obtaining command at an early age he remained at sea until his retirement in 1963 but sadly passed away in April 1964.

Captain W. Donald Pugsley hailing from Braunton commanded the tanker *"Saranac"* in the 1920s. Built in 1918 at Hebburn-on-Tyne and of 12,079 tons gross, this vessel was owned by the Anglo American Oil Co, and traded to Avonmouth.

Len Baglole left school in 1935 at 14 years of age and joined the *"Maude"* in the gravel trade to Bristol and coal trade back, before joining the *"Emily Barrett"* trading across to Ireland until the vessel was requisitioned by the Admiralty for war service about 1940. When he joined the *"Emily Barrett"* his pay was £3 per month, working 7 days a week and with no paid holidays. He also has been of immense help in the compiling of this book.

91. Len Baglole

Bill Crocker left school to join the ketch *"Agnes"* under Captain William (Bill) Mitchell before joining the *"Garlandstone"* and later the *"Crown of Denmark"*, which was operated by the Hunt family – Captain Walter Hunt and his brothers Charlie and Frank.

92. Bill Crocker

Whilst the *"Result"* is justifiably remembered as the last Braunton-owned vessel a similar vessel, the *"Eilian"* was operated by the Newcombe family who had an interest in her from 1923, when the she was managed by Sidney Incledon. She was sold by them in 1955 and after a further two difficult years in the coastal trade was finally sold abroad in 1957.

The Incledon family had extensive interests in local shipping, holding shares in a number of coasting ketches.

93. Captain Jack Newcombe (left) aboard "Eilian"

Sidney's brother, Captain Joe Incledon was master of the ketch *"Priory"* and his son Alfred Incledon was mate in the *"Bessie"* under Captain John Ayres before later becoming her skipper until 1950. His uncle, Fred Incledon, having initially been at sea, ran the local coal yard and imported coal into Velator Quay,

Sidney Incledon was the first local owner and master of the *"Result"*, who went to purchase the vessel and bring her to Braunton. Coming into Braunton Pill was always a narrow and tortuous passage and the local pilot who assisted vessels from Pillsmouth to Velator was Thomas Gideon Bassett. Vessels found some difficulty in getting to Velator until the coming of the auxiliary motor, following which designated moorings were laid by most vessels owners. Following Bassett's death Jan Crick of another seafaring family became the pilot for Braunton Pill and remained in this position until the end of the sailing ship era. Jan Crick was a man of many parts, being a seaweed gatherer, mussel picker, salmon fisherman and longshoreman for the area in addition to his pilotage duties.

94. Pilot Thomas Bassett at the helm of the ketch "Acacia" courtesy Joan Incledon

Jan Crick's father, Henry Abbot Crick went to sea on the *"Bessie Clarke"* aged 14 in 1887 and later had two sons – Sidney and John (known as Jan), both of whom went to sea in various Braunton vessels. Jan's son, also Jan, was a crew member of the *"Result"* in the 1950s.

The Drake and Corney families came from nearby Wrafton and Heanton, Captain Harry Drake being lost on the *"Mouse"* in 1916. Captain Bert Corney was master of the *"Morning Star"* which was armed as a "Q-ship" during the First World War. Captain Alf Corney, with his brothers Frank and Fred, had the *"William Martin"* and were aboard when it was sunk by a German submarine.

Captain Bob Parkhouse of the *"Lewisman"* was on a regular run between Port Talbot and Ilfracombe, and later had the *"Garlandstone"* and the *"Mary Stewart"* before retiring. His brother, Captain Alf Parkhouse joined the *"Margaret"* aged fifteen in 1908 and later the *"Amazon"* and *"TMP"* before spending a period in the Royal Navy and at sea with merchant steamships. He then bought the *"Clara May"* in 1923 and ran her until 1952 when he purchased *"Garlandstone"*.

Captain William Rogers of the *"Acacia"* owned the vessel for many years and operated in the flour trade in the Bristol Channel. He was killed in 1934 when helping to moor the *"Bessie Gould"* at Velator Quay. He was in the small boat when the *"Democrat"* entered under Captain Jack Chichester. She went astern but her engine was not powerful enough to get clear, and his head was crushed between the two boats and he died. After taking the matter to court his widow was finally awarded just £300 for the loss of her husband. His son, Stan Rogers had worked as mate with his father for over 20 years.

Stan's brother, Harold, also went to sea and joined the *"Emily Barratt"* before going into motor ships and working for Carters of Poole.

The Chichester family were related to the Chichesters' of Arlington Court, and the best remembered is Captain John Chichester who went to sea in a number of steamships from 1889-1892 before joining the *"Celtic Chief "*(seen left) for a passage to Australia. He returned to the coasting trade before becoming master of the *"Mary"* of Lynmouth. Being asked to sail on a Sunday was against his beliefs and he walked out. Purchasing the *"Lark"* and later the *"Julie"*, he had the *Bessie Ellen,* named after his daughters, built in 1906.

95. The ship "Celtic Chief"

In 1916 an auxiliary engine was installed and she continued in trade. On 4 May 1920 Captain John (Jack) Chichester was crushed between the side of the *"Bessie Ellen"* and a barge in Sharpness Lock after he secured his boat which was being towed, and he died from his injuries.. Captain Jack's son, also John was mate and thereafter took command, with George Stevens as crew.

Captain Reuben Chichester, John (senior) 's brother, was master of the engineless ketch *"Bonita",* and was known for rowing his vessel using large sweeps, when the wind and tide were suitable.

Captain Thomas Arthur Slee initially went deep-sea in square-riggers but during 40 years at sea served most of his time in Braunton vessels as A.B., mate and owner-captain. The vessels he sailed on included the *"Result", "Clara May", "Amazon", "Sultan"* and *"Bessie Clarke".* From there he joined *"Kitty Ann"* until 1922 when he bought a share in the *"Ann"*, running cargoes of coal to Lynmouth until 1930 when he established a coal store in Braunton.

Captain Robert Tucker of the *"Bessie Clarke"* carried cargoes of Lydney coal to Braunton where it was preferred for its burning properties. He had joined this vessel as an A.B. under Captain Harry Clarke after a period serving in various small sailing vessels, and remained in the vessel as mate and then master until he retired in 1942. He was known as a teetotaller, never leaving on a Sunday and always trying to be back in Braunton before Sunday.

Quite apart from the various masters, the seamen deserve mention as their tasks were all important in these lightly manned vessels working to a very tight budget. Very often they knew almost as much as the master. That they were not the skipper or owner/skipper was often due to lack of financial resources in those days of low pay and an inability to save the necessary monies for an investment of the amount required to own shares in a vessel.

Reg Williams, as an example, was mate in the *"Enid"* in the 1940s and was a thoroughly dependable and capable seaman, as well as being a first-class cook – any ship would have welcomed him. He was a practical man with vast experience but one would doubt that he held "paper" qualifications. Born about 1900, after working in the Post Office briefly in 1914 he joined the leaky *"Mary Grace"* for a few days before working on the *"Maggie Annie"*, and later the *"Troubadour"* and *"Henrietta"*. In 1916 he had tried to join the Navy but, because he had lost a finger at school, he was rejected. He was also refused when he tried to enlist in the Army so he joined the *"Marjorie"* under Captain Drake.

Reg Williams then joined the s.s. *"Harseywood"* at Newport taking coal to St. Nazaire and Bilbao, returning with iron ore. He then signed on to the ss *"War Firth"* in which he was torpedoed 4 September 1918, 33 miles S¾W of the Lizard, en route from Bilbao with iron ore bound for Glasgow. One boat was picked up with the survivors and taken to Penzance. When he returned home he was suffering from typhoid and dysentery. While convalescing at Heanton he saw the sailing coasters dressed overall – the War was over. After service deep-sea with merchant ships, he married and returned to Braunton where he signed on to the *"F.A.M.E."* She was subsequently lost on passage to Ilfracombe and he was fortunate to be picked up by the crew of the *"Lewisman"* in May 1929. He then joined the *"Bessie Ellen"* until 1934, when he moved to the *"Democrat"*. In 1936 he joined the *"Enid"* under Captain Bill Chichester, and later Captain Roland Chichester, where he stayed to the 1940s. Afterwards he sailed in the *"Olive Branch"*, *"Garlandstone"* and *"Mary Stewart"*, before completing his time on a barge plying between Bristol and Lydney. Such were the stuff of the crews of these vessels.

96. Reg Williams (Left) and Capt Bob Parkhouse aboard "Mary Stewart"

THE ON-GOING TRADITION

There are still men who whilst they did not serve in Braunton vessels still maintained the tradition of life at sea in various capacities

Brian Herniman, on the left, finished his education at Braunton school in 1969 and joined Reardon Smith & Sons Ltd's *"Devon City"* and later the *"Fresno City"*. Following their demise he moved to TMM with whom Reardons had forged strong ties. Gaining his Master's Certificate in 1980, when this Mexican company was taken over in 1988 by a German company, he moved to V-Ships of Southampton, a ship management company, and now works managing three cruise liners for Radisson Seven Seas Cruises for their subsidiary Celtic Pacific. Brian's father was a member of the *"Eilian's"* crew.

97. Brian Herniman

Roger Chugg, (see right) the great-great-grandson of Captain George Chugg and son of Captain Thomas Chugg, continued the family tradition over at least five generations when he joined the Sir William Reardon Smith line of cargo ships in 1970, and remained with them until their demise before joining P&O as an Electro Technical Officer. Reardon Smith was Appledore bred and had been an extra-master and captain in square rig, before settling in Cardiff where he established the Reardon Smith Shipping Company. He registered his ships at Bideford. He maintained a life-long connection with Appledore, sending £500 every Christmas to the deserving of Appledore, and a large 'Job Vacancy' was displayed in the post office when a vessel was being commissioned to enable local men to apply for work. Roger Chugg still retains his connection with sail, as he teaches sailing and has sailed the Atlantic and Far East as a Commercial Yachtmaster.

98. Roger Chugg

Richard Stanley Olden, (seen left), born in 1928 left Braunton to join Clan Line Steamship Company and the *"Clan Angus"* as a deck cadet. After joining the Union Castle Line in 1950 he became Staff Commander on their flagship *"Windsor Castle"* before being promoted as master of the *"Elizabeth Bowater"*. After commanding the *"Clan Graham"* he became cargo service representative for five shipping companies in Dar-es-Salaam Tanzania and finished his career as a consultant marine surveyor and assisting in various maritime legal issues.

99. Richard Olden

Thus it can be seen that Braunton, an unlikely place to nurture seamen, had over the years built up a firm tradition of seafaring families until the development of road transport in particular, saw the demise of coastwise local shipping. With the loss of the specialist skills to maintain and repair the vessels there are few alive now who would know how to sail these ships with a very small crew and heavy gear. Where two would be sufficient for a short run, today the *"Bessie Ellen"*, restored for recreational sailing, normally carries at least four crew to sail her – to say nothing of the 'willing' volunteers sailing for the experience.

100. The "Garlandstone" photographed by Dale Thomas, outside Swansea North Dock Basin on Saturday 20 September 1958. This was her last commercial trip to Swansea and she is seen lying empty waiting to go around to Port Talbot where she had been purchased by a plant hire operator for use as a yacht.
Courtesy Dale Thomas.

8. THE PIERHEAD PAINTINGS

DAVID CLEMENT

During the centuries of commercial sail the practice grew up of employing local artists to provide a painting of the vessel for purchase by the master and crew as a form of 'keepsake'. Some of these were comparatively primitive but by the end of the 19th. Century and into the early 20th. century – despite the advance of photography – the majority of paintings were generally architecturally correct and provided accomplished illustrations which today have become collectors pieces.

Because the artists would generally wait and approach the vessel at the arrival port many of the paintings show very similar scenes with the vessel painted onto a generally prepared background. Such artists worked worldwide with those in Malta, Italy and Antwerp well known. An example of an Italian artist is seen with the *"John Blackwell"*. Pierhead artists also practised in the United Kingdom and perhaps the best known and certainly the most prolific was Reuben Chappell, who was born in Goole in 1870 but later moved to Par in Cornwall in 1904, where a number of the westcountry schooners and ketches were regular visitors bringing coal in and carrying china clay from principally, the ports of Fowey and Par. Numerous paintings of the North Devon vessels survive as Reuben Chappell continued to paint until at least the 1930s (he died in 1940) and we therefore have accurate records illustrating the appearance of a number of the Braunton vessels.

101. Reuben Chappell 1870-1940
Courtesy Jean Dixon, (grand-daughter)

When comparing these to extant photographic illustrations, it is noteworthy just how accurate these paintings are seen to be. Reuben Chappell is considered to be one of the best of the pierhead painters. These works were generally supplied unframed, but were treasured by owners, masters, and, if they could afford to buy them, crew alike, and to this day are to be found in many North Devon homes as a reminder of the past.

A number of Reuben Chappell's paintings of Braunton vessels follow in this section. Another well-known pierhead painter was J. H. Harrison of Swansea who flourished in the early 20th. century. Since many of the Braunton vessels visited Swansea for coal or basic slag, illustrations of some appear in this section. A painting by Eric Voysey of Topsham who sailed in these vessels (the *"Julie"* of Braunton was sold to his father) and is an accomplished modern artist, is also included. Lastly we have examples of modern artists, the renowned Mark Myers and Brian Bale.

The section also contains photographic images by Jon Seagrave, the modern equivalent of a 'pierhead painter', of the *"Bessie Ellen"* for good measure.

102. A superb painting of the ketch "Agnes", seen in her later days complete with a wheelhouse by Mark Myers courtesy Bill Mitchell

103. The ketch *"Annie Christian"*, when she was owned in Watchet, later the Braunton *"Ade"*, painted by J. H. Harrison of Swansea.   *Courtesy Tom Welch*

104. The ketch "Bessie Clark", owned by George Clark of Braunton by an unknown artist. - Courtesy Des Tucker

105. A fine photograph of the "Bessie Ellen" powering along and now fully restored by Nicki Alford.
Photograph by Jon Seagrave

106. *"Bessie Ellen" practically becalmed in 2006. Photograph by Jon Seagrave.*

107. The ketch "Daring" built in 1863 at Bideford, Captain Frank Mitchell of Braunton, painted by Reuben Chappell.
Courtesy Sam Mitchell

108. A rough weather portrait of the schooner "Eilian" by Reuben Chappell courtesy P. Newcombe

109. The fine weather painting by Reuben Chappell, showing the schooner "Eilian" under full sail. With her stump bowsprit and topsails this painting shows her looking strangely unbalanced, but it is a truthful representation of her as Chappell was noted for accuracy. – Courtesy P. Newcombe

100

110. *A fine painting by Reuben Chappell of the ketch "Four Brothers"*
Courtesy Braunton Parish Council

111. Another 'rough' weather scene of the ketch "Four Brothers" painted by Reuben Chappell
Courtesy Braunton Parish Council

112. An Italian pierhead painter's view of the "John Blackwell" of Bideford, entering Naples in December 1864. She is reputed to have been crewed by Braunton men - Braunton Museum

103

113. The ketch "Julie" of Malpas, owned in her final days by the artist's father and painted by Eric Voysey of Topsham, who is a sailor with experience of these vessels.

114. The ketch "Lenora", owned by the Chichester family of Braunton from 1884 until she was wrecked in 1913, painted by J. H. Harrison. Courtesy Elizabeth Dyer

115. The schooner "Morning Star", Captain S. Corney, painted by Reuben Chappell
Courtesy Frank and Christine Skinner

116. *The ketch "Olive Branch", painted by Reuben Chappell.
Courtesy Braunton Parish Council*

117. The ketch "Pirate" of Barnstaple, owned by the Drake family for most of her working life, believed to be by J. H. Harrison
Courtesy John Hartnoll

118. The ketch "Priory" owned for most of her long life by the Incledon family of Braunton, believed to be by J. H. Harrison.
Courtesy Peter Incledon

119. The topsail schooner "Result" in her earlier days, painted by Reuben Chappell
Courtesy Sam Mitchell

120. A fine painting by the master, Reuben Chappell, of the "Result" as a three masted fore-and-aft schooner.
Courtesy Sarah Sankey

111

121. The second of the pair of Reuben Chappell paintings of the "Result" showing her in rough weather.
Courtesy Bob Andrew

122. The ketch "Rosie", built by Robert Cock at Appledore, seen in her later days, painted by Reuben Chappell
Courtesy Braunton Parish Council

123. The schooner "Rosie" of Appledore as originally built by Robert Cock, painted by Reuben Chappell
Courtesy Peter Ferguson

124. The ketch "St. Austell", painted by local artist Brian Bale. Courtesy Mark Mitchell

125. The schooner "Waterlily" owned by the Chugg family of Braunton from 1910, painted by Reuben Chappell. Courtesy Gail Sheppard

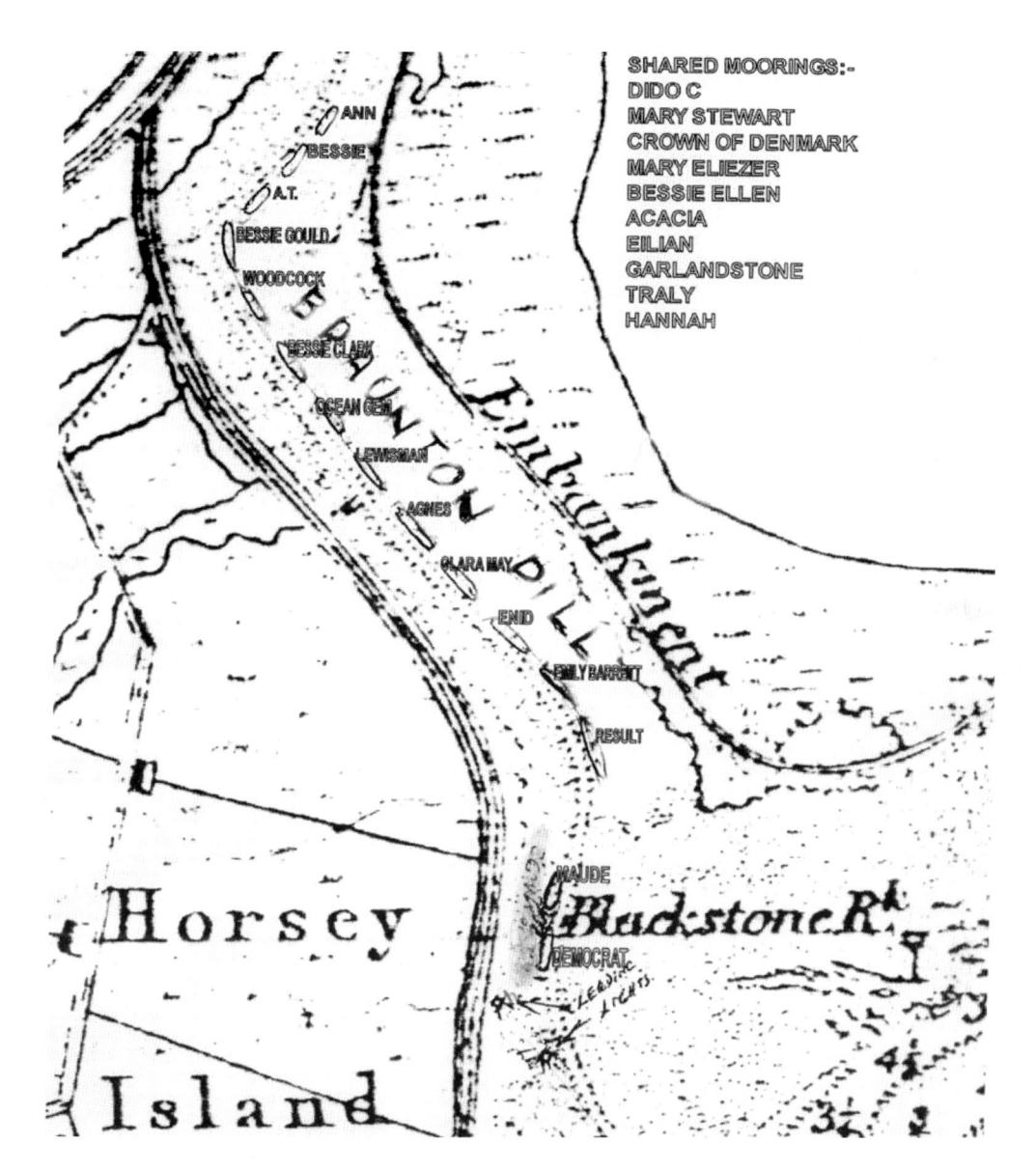

126. Braunton Pill showing the position of the moorings of the last 25 sailing coasters trading from there. The quayside at Velator was ½-mile upstream of the moorings on Braunton Pill. Before 1910 there were no moorings in Braunton Pill but with the coming of auxiliary engines vessels were able to access Braunton Pill for mooring purposes.

127. *Velator today with Big Quay (left), the slipway where cargoes of seaweed were unloaded, and Little Quay to the right, now a haven for pleasure craft. Courtesy Andrew Byrom.*

9 – BRAUNTON VESSELS

ACACIA Smack, later ketch

Built: Banks & Co Plymouth, 1880
Official Number: 81036
First Owner: 1880, David Banks
1885 Re-rigged as a Ketch
Second Owner: 1893 William T. Rogers
MFSM

Signal Hoist: TDVJ
Signal Hoist:

60.5ft. x 18.6 x 7.4
19.85m. x 6.10 x 2.42
NRT: 45
Registered: Plymouth

Registered: Barnstaple

William Rogers was killed at Velator Quay around 1930, when he was crushed trying to save his ship from being damaged by another vessel coming alongside with too much way on. He jumped into the ship's boat and was struck by the offending vessel. Mrs. Rogers sold the vessel to John Ford, a local Pembroke garage owner.

Third Owner: 1931, John Ford, Pembroke   Registered: Barnstaple

Broken up 1947

128. "Acacia" beating out of the estuary around 1906, with Braunton Lighthouse behind.
Photo courtesy Braunton Museum.

129. A spot of tender care - Captain William Rogers and George Dendle tarring the bottom of "Acacia" at Appledore in 1906. – Braunton Museum

119

130. "Acacia" on the hard at Braunton Pill
Bill Mitchell

131."Acacia" – deck scene with Captain William Rogers
Bill Mitchell

120

Built: W. Westacott	**ANNIE CHRISTIAN**	76.5ft. x 20.5 x 9
Barnstaple, 1881	Signal Hoist: JCFH	25.09m. x 6.72 x 2.95
Official Niumber: 76819	Schooner	NRT 69
First Owner: Edward QUAYLE, Ramsey, Isle of Man		Registered: Ramsey

In 1888 she was sunk in collision. Her cargo of beans swelled and burst through her decks and after being salvaged a new deck was required and she was re-rigged as a ketch being sold eventually to Watchet owners.

Second Owner: Registered: Liverpool
Third Owner: 1890, Isaac ALLEN, 7, Portland Terrace, Watchet   Registered: Liverpool

1891 lying at Charlestown the Census shows: the ship arrived from Liverpool with Isaac Allen, master aged 48; John Short, aged 52, mate; Henry John Norman, aged 21, Ordinary Seaman and Arthur Davis, aged 15, Boy all employed at and from Watchet, Somerset. He still owned her in 1912.

Fourth Owner: Somerset Trading Company, Bridgwater   Registered: Bridgwater
                                   Renamed **ADE**   NRT: 52
                              Signal Hoist: MDXF
                                          Ketch

Fifth Owner: 1930 Philip W. HARRIS, Appledore   Registered: Bideford,
Sixth Owner: John AYRE, Braunton   Registered: Bideford
                           Broken up at Appledore 1946

132/3. The fine ketch "Ade" seen left on Appledore beach and above having discharged a cargo of coal – both photographs courtesy Mark Myers.

134. The Ketch "Ade" leaving Lynmouth in 1934 – Mark Myers

Built: J & W Francis
   Pembroke, Milford Haven, 1893
Official Number:99999
Owner: Frederick Joseph INCLEDON, Braunton

ADVANCE
Signal Hoist: NFKH
Ketch
Lost St. Georges Channel, 1906

71.7ft. x 19.3 x 8.6
23.52m. x6.33 x 2.82
NRT 59
Registered: Milford

Built: Rudland Brothers
   Bude, 1904
Official Number: 105246
Owner: Nicholas H. Tregaskes, Bude
Second Owner: Frederick R. E. WRIGHT, Braunton
Third Owner: H. Clarke and W Mitchell, Braunton
Fourth Owner: 1955, Captain Peter Herbert, Bude

AGNES   Ketch
Signal Hoist:

Sold out of trade in 1957 and Wrecked Barbados, 1958

70.6ft. x 18.5 x 8.0
23.16 x 6.07 x 2.62
NRT: 54
Registered: Bideford
Registered: Bideford
Registered: Bideford
Registered: Bideford

135/6. "Agnes" owned by Captain Peter Herbert of Bude, loading wheat feed at Barry in 1955 – Bill Mitchell

137. The ketch "Agnes" stranded at Kinsale, Ireland in 1919.
Braunton Museum

138. "Agnes" leaving Bude, in 1935 light for Lydney, and another cargo of coal – Bill Mitchell

139. The "Agnes" sailing inside the Nash Sands – Bill Mitchell

140. Porthclain Harbour, St. Davids with the ketch "Agnes" discharging. This gives an idea of how difficult the entrance was to many of these small shelters that these vessels were called upon to visit. – Bill Mitchell from a commercial illustration

141. The "Agnes" discharging at Rolle Quay, Barnstaple 25 August 1949 – Bill Mitchell

142. "Agnes" discharging coal at Bude in 1937 – Bill Mitchell

125

Built: **ALERT** Smack 36.6ft x
1823 Signal Hoist: None 12.00m. x
Official Number: None NRT: 20
Owned in Braunton from 1841 Transferred to Barnstaple Registry, 1841

Built: J. & W. Francis ?Allen? **ALFRED & EMMA** Smack 69.5ft. x 19.7 x 9.0
Pembroke Dock, Signal Hoist: None 22.80m. x 6.46 x 2.95
Milford Haven, 1861 NRT: 67
Signal Hoist: PSJB
Official Number: 27961
First Owner: Allen & Co. Note: *Lloyds, 1861- Shown as "Schooner" built Allen*
Registered: Milford
Second Owner: 1880, Edwin QUALTROUGH, Port St. Mary, Isle of Man Registered: Castletown
Third Owner: 1901, Henry CLARKE,(mgr.), Thomas CLARKE, and Registered Barnstaple
William PARKHOUSE, of Braunton.
Altered 1922 when an engine was fitted and she may have been converted to a ketch. NRT: 58
Stranded on Saunton Sands and wrecked, 1922

143. The "Alfred & Emma" seen entering the tiny harbour of Porthgain.
Photo – Braunton Museum

	AMAZON Ketch	65.5ft. x 16.3 x 8.2
Built: Le Sueur	Signal Hoist: None	21.49m. x 5.35 x 2.69
Jersey, 1866		NRT 50
Official Number: 55266		Registered: Jersey

First Owner: J. WRIGHT
Second Owner: 1870, James RICHMOND Lengthened from original build
                                                                                                                      Registered: Jersey
Third Owner: 1904, James WATTS, East Street, Braunton   Registered: Barnstaple
Fourth Owner: 1924, A. W. CORNEY, Seabourne Villas, Braunton   Registered: Barnstaple
                  Auxiliary engine fitted 1927   NRT 34
Fifth Owner: 1927, Oscar A. HARRIS, 85 Sea View, Par   Registered: Barnstaple
                                Vessel lost 1936

	AMY Ketch	86ft. x 20.7 x 11.4
Built: Watson,	Signal Hoist: PBSJ	28.21m. x 6.79 x 3.74
Banff, 1870		NRT: 51
Official Number: 62443		

First Owner: William SIMPSON, Grant Street, Inverness   Registered: Inverness
Second Owner: Registered: Newcastle
Third Owner: Mrs. J. WILLCOCKS, Calstock   Registered: Fowey
Fourth Owner: 1926, A. WESTCOTT, Braunton   Registered: Fowey
        Master: Captain J. H. Greet, Crewmember: Jan Crick

	ANN Ketch	59ft.2ins. x
Built: William Date,	Signal Hoist: None	19.41m. x
Kingsbridge, 1889		NRT 47
Official Number: 86469		

First Owner: William Edward HURDLE, Topsham   Registered: Salcombe
Second Owner: 1920, Thomas A SLEE (Mgr), Claude CHUGG, Braunton Registered: Salcombe
     15hp auxiliary engine installed 1920, and NRT reduced. NRT: 33
Owned by above until at least 1934 and thereafter owned in Combe Martin.

144. "Ann"of Salcombe, discharging coal brought from Lydney, at Lynmouth in 1924
– photo Tom Welch

145. The "Ann" of Salcombe, her deep narrow hull seen to advantage at Velator. The two crewmen are fixing the stirrups on the rigging of the foremast. Photo – Tom Welch

146. "Ann", discharging Lydney coal at Velator – photo Braunton Museum

147. Cargo handling aboard the "Ann" in 1927, discharging sand and gravel. Note the large wicker baskets used for handling the cargo, which were called "maunds". Photo Tom Welch

148. Ketch "Ann" discharging into a lorry on the beach at Combe Martin – Bill Mitchell

149. A moody photograph of the "Ann" lying off Appledore, in 1941 when commanded by Captain Jim Screech – Courtesy Peter Herbert

Built: J. & W. Francis	**A.T.** **Ketch**	62ft. x 18.0 x 7.0
Milford Haven, 1894	Signal Hoist: None	20.34m x 5.91 x 2.29
Official Number: 104112		NRT. 36
First Owner: Thomas THOMAS, Ddol, Aberpoth, Cardigan		Registered: Barnstaple
Second Owner: Henry REDMORE, South Street, Braunton		nrt 30, grt 40 from 1925

Ida CHILCOTT, Francis CLOGG
Named after "Anne Thomas" she traded out of Barnstaple from 1914. Engine fitted 1925. Sold 1938. Broken up at Angle, Milford Haven, 1950

*150. "A.T." seen at Bude –
courtesy Tom Welch*

151. "A.T", Running free – courtesy Peter Herbert

Built: J & W Francis
    Pembroke Dock, Milford Haven
    1900
    Official Number 112455

BESSIE   Ketch 59.4ft. x 18.2 x 6.7
Signal Hoist: None   19.49m. x 5.97 x 2.19
   NRT: 34

First Owner: John GEORGE, Trevine, Pembroke   Registered: Milford
Second Owner: 1911 Frederick J. INCLEDON (mgr), Sid INCLEDON,   Registered: Barnstaple
H. G. G. Clarke, Kate Irene COLLINS, E. J. SLEE, John AYRE
Miss L. CHUGG, all of Braunton. Master: John AYRE.
Auxiliary engine fitted 1913 and NRT reduced   NRT: 28
Sold out of trade in 1946 and lost 1951 at Jeddah in the Red Sea.

152. The "Bessie" lying at Velator, Braunton.
Photo by Tom Welch

153. Below, we see the deep-laden "Bessie" lying outside Sully & Co's premises waiting to leave Lydney with another cargo of coal.
Courtesy Braunton Museum

133

154. The "Bessie" lying empty at Bude having discharged coal in 1937 – Bill Mitchell

Built: H. M. Restarick **BESSIE CLARKE** Ketch 59.1ft. x 18.2 x 7.5
    Bideford, 1881   Signal Hoist: None   19.39m. x 5.97 x 2.46
    Official Number: 84471   NRT: 44
First Owner: George Clarke, Braunton   Registered: Barnstaple
    The first Braunton vessel to be fitted with an auxiliary engine in 1909.
Second Owner: Henry S. G. Clarke, Braunton   Registered: Barnstaple
    Broken up at Appledore 1945/6 following war service as a Barrage Balloon vessel.

155. Captain Tom A. Slee 1934 (above)
— Braunton Museum

156. The "Bessie Clark" (right) at Velator. Photo — Robert Andrew

157. The "Bessie Clark" lying at Porlock waiting to discharge her cargo of coal — Bill Mitchell

135

158. The "Bessie Clark" lying at Velator, Braunton waiting for the tide. – Braunton Museum

159. Lying at Rolle Quay, Barnstaple outside W. Dalling & Sons' coal stores are the ketches "Bessie Clark"(left), the "Ocean Gem" (centre) and the "Lewisman" (right). The vessel forward of the "Bessie Clark" has not been positively identified. – Bill Mitchell

Built: William S. Kelly	**BESSIE ELLEN**	Ketch	77.4ft. x 20.1 x 9.5
Mountbatten, Plymouth, 1907	Signal Hoist: HKCM		25.39m. x 6.59 x 3.12
Official Number: 120098			NRT: 60

Built on speculation and intended for the Newfoundland salt fish trade she was named after the two daughters of her managing owner: Bessie and Ellen.

First Owner: John Squire CHICHESTER (Mgr.), Bessie Gould   Registered: Barnstaple
           CHICHESTER, Reuben CHICHESTER and George
           CLARKE of East Street, Braunton.

1910 – ran aground on Morte Stone, but salvaged and taken to Appledore for repairs.
1916 25hp. Auxiliary Widdup oil engine installed and NRT reduced   NRT: 57

Renamed: FORSØGET (Danish flag)

Second Owner: 1947, Capt. Christian Moller, Fredriksvaerk, Denmark
               Her name means "Endeavour". Used in the scrap metal trade
               until 2000 with Hundestead oil engine installed.   Registered: Fredriksvaerk

Third Owner: 1980 Ole Pieterson

Purchased with the intention of restoration but laid up at Svendborg in the J. Ring Andersen Yard.

Renamed BESSIE ELLEN (British flag)

Fourth Owner: 2000, Nikki ALFORD   Registered: Plymouth
                                                                                  GRT: 87

Auxiliary 310hp Volvo Penta diesel installed. Refitted from 2000 until 2002, since when she has been used as a charter vessel with berths for 20 persons, initially based at Plymouth and currently (2007) in Denmark.

160. "Bessie Ellen" lying off Burnham in 1937 – James Dew

161. *"Bessie Ellen" under full sail departing from Ramsey Harbour, 1909 – Braunton Museum*

2. The crew of "Bessie Ellen" in 1920, with Bill Bray, Jack Chichester, John Watt and Reg Williams – Braunton Museum

163. "Bessie Ellen" at Bristol in 1911, with John Chichester and Charlie Mitchell
Braunton Museum

Built: William Westacott,
    Barnstaple, 1872
    Official Number: 68197
First Owner: George CHUGG, 16/64ths (Mgr.) George CHUGG, Arthur
    CHUGG of Braunton
Auxiliary oil engine fitted 1914 and NRT reduced.
Second Owner: 1930, Henry S. G. CLARKE, East Hill, Braunton
    Broken up 1936

BESSIE GOULD   Ketch
Signal Hoist: None

65.3ft. x 20.5 x 7.9
21.42m. x 6.73 x 2.59
NRT: 48
Registered: Barnstaple
NRT: 42
Registered: Barnstaple

164. The "Bessie Gould" laden with basic slag in the entrance to Bude on 14 April 1936. Note the arm to the sea lock entrance gates to the extreme left. – Bill Mitchell

165. "Bessie Gould" loading gravel on Crow Gravel Ridge in 1920, with (left to right) George John Irwin, George Coates, Herbie Hartnall Shadda, Bill Mullern, Tom 'Nappa' Philips, George Parkins, Harry Riddal; Sitting: Frank 'Daddy' Bowhill, and 'Liberty' Bert Irwin; with on the rail Captain Fred Williams and George John Irwin. The dog was called Shep.
Photo courtesy Braunton Museum

Built: William Westacott   **BESSIE WATERS** Ketch   63.8ft. x 19.5 x 8.7
     Barnstaple, 1871   Signal Hoist: None   20.93m. x 6.40 x 2.85
     Official Number: 62864   NRT: 51
First Owner: J. WATERS   Registered: Padstow
Second Owner: 1881, Frederick Samuel PIERCE   Registered: Dover
Third Owner: 1891, Mrs Catherine PIERCE (Frederick CRUNDALL Mgr.) Registered: Dover
In the Mercantile Navy List there is no trace of two separate vessels carrying this name, only that built by Westcott in 1871. There is similarly no trace of William Rafarel in the Mercantile Navy Lists.
Owner: William Claude RAFAREL, Corfe Green, Braunton.   Registered: Barnstaple

There is something of a mystery as a BESSIE WATERS, owned by Catherine Pierce, and built by Westacott, was lost at Lower Hope in the Thames on 10 September 1891 following a collision with the ss HARTSIDE of Newcastle-on-Tyne. We do not know whether the vessel was salvaged but BESSIE WATERS registered at Barnstaple was lost in a force 12 westerly gale off Shoreham-by-Sea, whilst on passage in ballast from Caen to Appledore. She was stated to be then owned by W. Lemon of Barnstaple and sank 21 December 1893. William Rafarel could have been a shareholder in the vessel at that time.

Built: Le Sueur   **BONITA**   Ketch   57.9ft. x 16.1 x 7.4
     Jersey, 1881   Signal Hoist: WDCR   18.99m. x 5.28 x 2.43
     Official Number: 76278   NRT: 37
First Owner: John Charles RENOUF, 20, Cheapside, St. Helier   Registered: Jersey
Second Owner: 1905, Reuben CHICHESTER, Church Street, Braunton
     Registered: Barnstaple
     Signal Hoist changed to MPFB
Lost 1st August 1934 off Barry, still without an auxiliary engine.

166. The ketch "Bonita" sailing past Instow off Appledore – Appledore Museum

167. A dramatic photograph showing the loss of the ketch "Bonita" near Barry, South Wales on 1 August 1934 – Jean McDine

Built: James Goss	**C.F.H.** Ketch	74ft. x 20.4 x 9.3
Calstock, 1892	Signal Hoist: MQKN	24.28m. x 6.69 x 3.05
Official Number: 99268		NRT: 71

Named after a member of William Hamley's family, Charles Francis HOBSON. Hamleys were timber merchants of Bere Alston and Plymouth, and the *C.F.H.* was built from timber blown down in the great blizzard of 12 March 1891 from the Cotehele Estate. In terms of cargo capacity she was the largest vessel built by James Goss.

First Owner: William H. HAMLEY, 1, Portland Square, Plymouth
                                                                                             Registered: Plymouth
Second Owner: 1911, Breton Group of traders   Registered: St. Brieuc, Brittany
Third Owner   1914, Harry G. G. CLARKE, 20, Hills View, Braunton
                 Other shareholders were John CLARKE, Francis
                 WELCH, and Lilian CHUGG   Registered: Barnstaple

Chartered by the Admiralty as a Fleet Tender in Scapa Flow during the 1914-18 War.
An auxiliary oil engine fitted and NRT reduced   NRT: 56
Resumed trading to Lydney and in Bristol Channel and Irish trades from 1918.
Fourth Owner: 1952, William SCREECH   Registered: Barnstaple
Hulked 1953

168.   The "C.F.H." seen at Penarth in 1939.
Braunton Museum

169.   The crew of "C.F.H." seen at Velator around 1930.
Braunton Museum

170. Ilfracombe before the 1939/45 War with the three-masted schooner "M. A. James" in the foreground and the ketch "C.F.H." lying behind. In the distance Starkey's (now a part of Whitbreads) White Hart Hotel can be made out with the offices of P. & A. Cambell, the operators of the paddle steamer service to Swansea and Cardiff to their left.
Appledore Museum

	CAMBRIA Smack	50.1ft. x 16.5 x 8.0
Built: Rees & Co		
Llanelly, 1851	Signal Hoist: MLKR	16.44m. x 5.41 x 2.62
Official Number: 18356		NRT: 40
First Owner: T. Rees & Co.		Registered: Llanelly

By 1860 she was unclassed and no longer listed in Lloyd's Register, although apparently still in trade for Rees & Co. She may have had another owner who registered her at Milford before she passed to Chichester.

Second Owner: By 1884, John CHICHESTER, Braunton Converted to a ketch
                                                                                                                     Registered: Milford
                1885, John CHICHESTER, Braunton   Registered: Barnstaple
                                                                                                               NRT:39
Third Owner: 1896, Ellen CHICHESTER, Braunton (widow)   Registered: Barnstaple
                                                                                                                         NRT:39
Fourth Owner: 1903, Henry CHICHESTER   Registered: Barnstaple
                             Foundered in Bristol Channel 1905

Built: Not determined   **CELIA**   Ketch   42.5ft. x 16.0 x 6.5
     Llanelly, 1851   Signal Hoist: None   13.94m. x 5.25 x 2.13
     Official Number: 10834   NRT: 25
First Owner:
Second Owner: 1857,   Registered: Barnstaple
Third Owner: 1869, George LAMPREY, Braunton 64/64 shares   Registered: Barnstaple

Built: Langley   **CHARLOTTE**   Ketch   77ft. x 18.8 x 9.7
     Southampton, 1864   Signal Hoist: VQWF   25.26m. x 6.17 x 3.18
     Official Number: 47989   NRT 77
First Owner: G. LANGLEY   Registered: Southampton
Second Owner: 1867, W. JOHNSON   Registered: Goole
     NRT: 84
Third Owner: 1880, Rhodes HUDSON, 34, Vermuyden Terrace, Goole   Registered: Goole
Fourth Owner: 1890, Mrs Anne DAVIS, Watchet   Registered: Goole
Fifth Owner: 1900, William J NORMAN, Watchet   Registered: Goole
     NRT: 69
Sixth Owner: 1905, The Wansborough Paper Co Ltd., Watchet   Registered: Goole
Owned by Wansborough Paper Co. until at least 1920 she was out of the Register by 1934 but we are advised was owned by BUTLER of Braunton in the late 1920s.

Built: Watson & Fox   **CLARA MAY**   Ketch   75.9ft. x 19.7 x 8.9
     Plymouth, 1891   Signal Hoist: RBKD   24.90m. x 6.46 x 2.92
     Official Number: 99255   NRT: 73
First Owner: 1899, J. REED, Metropole Hotel, Bournemouth   Registered: Plymouth
Owner: 1902, John J. CORNISH, Bude View, Bude   Registered: Plymouth
She may have had an engine fitted as her NRT significantly reduced about 1909 - NRT: 60
An auxiliary engine was also fitted in 1926.
Owner: 1934, Alfred PARKHOUSE, Arlington Terrace, Braunton
     and H. G. S. CLARKE   Registered: Plymouth
     NRT: 52
She was hulked at Velator, Braunton 1952 following damage at Fremington, when she was sold out of trade.

171. The "Clara May" at Pill, 1939
Photo – Braunton Museum

172. The "Clara May" lying at Velator
Appledore Museum

173. "Clara May" approaching Bude, 1910 – photo Braunton Museum

174. The "Clara May" off Appledore, about 1935, Capt. Alf Parkhouse – Braunton Museum

Built: T. Waters   **COMET** Smack
    Guernsey, 1842   Signal Hoist: LJVC
    Official Number: 13842   NRT: 33
First Owner: T. WATERS   Registered: Guernsey
By 1884 she had been converted to a ketch and was registered in Southampton
Owner: From 1884 to 1889, James S. LEWIN, Exeter   Registered: Southamtpon
     NRT: 58
Stated to be owned by H REDMORE, Braunton   Registered: Southampton
By 1889 she is not listed in the Mercantile Navy Lists.
     Lost off Lands End 1891

Built: O. Smit   **CROWN OF DENMARK** Ketch   101.6ft. x 19.1 x 8.5
     Stadskanaal (Holland), 1918   Signal Hoist: MKNC   33.33m. x 6.27 x 2.79
     Official Number: 145111   Built of steel   NRT: 102
     Previously named **AUTO**, ex-**AFIENA MARCHIENA**
Owners: 1925, Heywood Brothers, Exeter   Registered: London
Owners: 1934, Walter R. HUNT, Abbotscliff, Braunton   Registered: London
     Sold 1946 to Danish owners and renamed **DEJRO**

175. The steel motor ketch "Crown of Denmark" at sea – Tom Welch

Built: John Johnson   **DARING**   Dandy   69.4ft. x 18.0 x 8.1
     Bideford, 1863   Signal Hoist: QHJM   22.77m. x 5.90 x 2.66
     Official Number: 29843   NRT: 48
First Owner: 1863, J, MILLS, Bideford   Registered: Bideford
Second Owner: 1866, Richard BAMENT, Barnstaple   Registered: Barnstaple
Third Owner: 1881-1889, Mrs. Helena M. BAMENT, Barnstaple
                                                                               Registered: Barnstaple
                 Frank Mitchell, from Braunton, sailed as mate
Fourth Owner: 1891, Charles W. PRICE , Newport, Isle of Wight   Registered: Cowes
                                Converted to a ketch
Fifth Owner: 1920, Vectis Shipping Co. Ltd, Newport   Registered: Guernsey
Sixth Owner: 1921, James Slade, Appledore   Registered: Guernsey
                                 Out of Register by 1928

176. The ketch "Daring" at Appledore about 1922.- Mark Myers

See also the illustration in the colour section.

Built   **DASHER**   Smack
     Bideford, 1832   Signal Hoist: None
     Official Number: 15512   NRT: 22
First Owner: J. SQUIRES   Registered: Bideford
Second Owner: 1861, DRAKE, HAMLYN & TANCOCK   Registered: Barnstaple
Third Owner: 1884, William DAVIES, Rhoscribed, St. Davids, Pembroke.
                                                          Registered: Barnstaple
                             Broken up 1889

Built: Padstow   **DELABOLE**   Smack   49ft. 8ins
     1826   Signal Hoist: None   16.29m.
     Official Number: None   NRT: 52
Owned: 1834, Dyer & Co. (Captain Tuckfield)   Registered: Barnstaple
Major repairs were carried out to the vessel in 1832, when she was continued 10years A1. At this time she was rigged as a schooner.
                                  Lost 1837

Built: J. & W. Francis   **DEMOCRAT**   Ketch   71.2ft. x 19.0 x 7.7
     Castle Pill,   Signal Hoist: None   23.36m. x 6.23 x 2.53
     Milford Haven, 1909   NRT: 48
     Official Number: 120099   Sistership to the EDITH (qv)
First Owner: Henry S. G. CLARKE, East Hill, Braunton   Registered: Barnstaple
     Other Shareholders: George CLARKE, Thomas
         Clarke WELCH of Braunton and James Thomas WELCH, Simonsbath.
             An auxiliary engine was fitted in 1912
                       Sold out of trade in 1954

177. The ketch "Democrat" ghosts along through Milford Haven
Braunton Museum

178. "Democrat" in Velator Pool – Tom Welch

179. "Democrat" (left) lying in Bude Canal – Appledore Museum

180. A busy scene at Rolle Quay, Barnstaple, with the ketches "Democrat"(right) and from front to back, "Enid", Mary Stewart", "Bessie", "Ocean Gem" and "Maude" outside Stanbury's Mills. - Braunton Museum

Built	**DIDO C.** Ketch	74.7ft. x 20.9 x 7.4
Lysekie, Sweden, 1921	Signal Hoist: None	24.51m. x 6.85 x 2.43
Official Number: 148211		NRT: 41

Built as the JULE CLAES

Owner: 1924, Stephen G. B. CHUGG, Franklin House, Braunton

Registered: Barnstaple

Sold 1942 to Scottish owners

151

181/2. The auxiliary ketch "Dido C." at Velator Quay, in 1939.

Braunton Museum

183. "Dido C." discharging coal on Bryher, Isles of Scilly about 1930
Charmian Astbury

184. A spectacular photograph of the "Dido C.", grounded on the Morte Stone, in 1936. Fortunately she was floated off comparatively undamaged on the rising tide. Courtesy R. L. Knight.

Built: James Goss	**DISPATCH** Smack	49.5ft. x 14.2 x 7.0
Barnstaple, 1852	Signal Hoist: None	16.24m. x 6.66 x 2.30
Official Number: 1678		NRT: 36

First Owner: 1852-1869, W. SANDERS, Barnstaple   Registered: Barnstaple
(Master: R. Bament)
Second Owner: R BAMENT, Braunton   Registered: Barnstaple
Third Owner: 1884-1891, Mrs. Mary BAMENT, Quay Place. Registered: Barnstaple
Re-rigged as a Ketch during the 1880s.
Fourth Owner: 1905-12, John COX, 34, Market Street, Appledore
    Registered: Barnstaple

There is mention of a PADDISON as a Braunton owner, but he may have been a shareholder.

Entry deleted from Mercantile Navy List by 1914

Built: John Chappell,	**DOVE** Brig	
Pilton, Barnstaple, 1822	Signal Hoist: None	NRT: 35
Official Number: 15316		
Owner: William Drake, Braunton		Registered: Barnstaple

Built: J. & W. Francis,   **EDITH**   Ketch   67.4ft. x 18.9 x 7.6
    Castle Pill,   Signal Hoist: None   22.11m. x 6.20 x 2.49
    Milford Haven, 1906   NRT: 45
    Official Number: 121611

Sistership of the DEMOCRAT (q.v.) although slightly smaller.
First Owner: 1906, J. & W. FRANCIS, Milford Haven.   Registered: Milford
Second Owner: 1909, John CLARKE, Wrafton and H. G. CLARKE, Braunton
              with Ann CLARKE of Wrafton.   Registered: Barnstaple
In 1910, became the second Braunton vessel to be fitted with an auxiliary engine.
Sunk 1912 in the Bristol Channel following collision with the ss THIRLBY resulting in the mate being drowned and the master and boy saved.

Built: William Thomas & Sons   **EILIAN**   Schooner   102.6ft. x 21.9 x 8.4
    Amlwch, Anglesey, 1908   Signal Hoist: HNJR   33.66m. x 7.18 x 2.75
    Official Number: 127943   NRT: 80

Built as a steel three pole masted schooner and the first to be launched fitted with a 50hp 2 cylinder Kromhaut paraffin engine.
First Owner: David RICHARDSON, Rock Park, Rock Ferry, Cheshire.
            (W. Thomas & Sons, mgrs.)   Registered: Liverpool
Second Owner: 1910, C. W. MARSHALL, (W. Thomas & Sons mgrs.)
                                    Registered: Liverpool
            1915-1917 Chartered by Admiralty for service as a 'Q'-ship.
Second Owner: 1923, Sidney J. INCLEDON, (mgr.) William DRAKE,
        George Perryman HARTNOLL,(master)
           John NEWCOMBE   Registered: Barnstaple
Owned from October 23 1923, Captain Newcombe succeeded to command on the retirement of George Hartnoll in March 1934.
Third Owner   1934-1957 John NEWCOMBE (mgr.)   Registered: Barnstaple
Fourth Owner: 1955, Holger P. ASSMUSSEN   Registered Barnstaple
    Remained in the coastal trade of the UK until 1957
                    Renamed   **HOAN** (Danish)
    1957, Holger P. ASSMUSSEN   Registered: Egernsund
Fifth Owner: 1970, Aage Poulsen Partrederi   Registered: Ålborg
                  Renamed **KAMINA** (Danish)
Following capsizing and sinking the vessel was salvaged and sold for refurbishment.
Sixth Owner: 1976, Roar B.H. NIELSEN   Registered: Ålborg
                 Renamed **FJORDBO** (Danish)
Seventh Owner: 1977, Paul Jensen   Registered: Copenhagen
Eighth Owner: 1978, Earl Byron CLARKE, Barbados.   Registered: Barbados
Ninth Owner: 1983, John Arthur St. CLAIR   Registered: Castries, St. Lucia
                    Renamed **IDA S.** (St. Lucia)
The vessel continued in trade carrying cargoes around the West Indies until she foundered on a voyage about the 9 January 1984. She took on water about 110 km north east of the Venezuelan island of La Orchila and instead of making for this landfall, voyaged a further 183 km to the north west, before foundering. Perhaps she was on route to Kingston, Jamaica which lay about a further 1200 km to the north west and on same heading from where she sank in about 5000 metres of water.
On 6th January the Venezuelan Navy frigate *ALMIRANTE BRION* (Γ22) was reported

standing by the auxiliary motor schooner *IDA S* in latitude 12 21N longitude 65 15W. Her crew of four had abandoned ship as she had been taking on water rapidly and had a thirty-degree list. The crew were rescued by another vessel that proceeded with them to Puerto Rico.

185. The schooner "Eilian" lying in Ilfracombe – Mark Myers

186. Under full sail, the "Eilian" makes a fine picture – Bill Mitchell

187. In an almost dead calm, the schooner "Eilian", deep laden with coal for the local gasworks, enters Ilfracombe.   Appledore Museum

188. A lovely photograph which shows the lines of the "Eilian" to perfection.
Mark Myers

	ELIZA Smack	42.6ft. x 15.4 x 6.7
Built:		
Milford Haven, 1830	Signal Hoist: None	13.98m. x 5.05 x 2.19
Official Number: 15808		NRT: 25
Owner: 1839,		Registered: Bideford
Owner: 1864, Henry DRAKE of Braunton		Registered: Barnstaple

ELIZA ANNE Ketch

Built:
    Quayback, Cardigan, 1877 Signal Hoist: None
    Official Number: 69853   NRT: 32
Owner: 1884-1906, David EVANS, St. Dogmaels   Registered: Cardigan
Owner: 1912-1914, John EVANS, Gladegwal, St. Dogmaels Registered: Cardigan
Understood to have been briefly owned by G. CLARKE of Braunton after 1915.
                Out of Mercantile Navy List by 1920

ELIZA ANNIE Schooner   81.1ft. x 27.2 x 10.4

Built: C. Rawle,
    Padstow, 1876 Signal Hoist: QKGN   24.72m. x 8.29 x 3.17
Official Number: 74625   NRT: 96
First Owner: J. Hambly, Calstock   Registered: Plymouth
Second Owner: 1899, Henry Clarke, Braunton, and Ann Clarke 16/64
                                                            Registered: Plymouth
Purchased 6 March 1899, she stranded in Glandore Bay, Co. Cork 6 miles south of Clonakilty with a crew of 4 on passage Newport, Mon to Ballynacurra with coal, driven ashore by wind force 7 and tide on 30 December 1899 and was a total loss.

Built: Thomas Evans   **ELIZABETH**   Ketch   50.1ft. x 14.7 x 6.7
    Cleave Houses, Bideford   Signal Hoist: None   16.44m. x 4.82 x 2.19
    1837   NRT: 22
    Official Number: 15324

Built as a smack she was lengthened and re-rigged as a ketch, 1859

Owner: 1859, Incledon HARRIS 64/64, Braunton   Registered: Barnstaple
Owner: 1884, John HEDDON, Braunton   Registered: Barnstaple
                                                                       NRT: 29

Out of Mercantile Navy List by 1906

Built: Gough & Moulton   **ELIZABETH**   Ketch   59.7ft. x 18.5 x 7.5
    Bridgwater, 1854   Signal Hoist: KQHR   19.59m. x 6.07 x 2.46
    Official Number: 10886   NRT: 47

First Owner: Previous history not determined   Registered: Bridgwater
First Owner: 1884 John Bryant, Bridgwater   Registered: Bridgwater
Second Owner: 1906, Robert S. ROBERTS, Brynderwen Road, Newport
                                                                       Registered: Bridgwater
Second Owner: 1912, Robert DRAKE, Wrafton Road, Braunton
                                                                        Registered: Barnstaple

Altered 1920, and converted to a lighter in 1928.

189. The ketch "Elizabeth" seen about 1914 – Bill Mitchell

	ELIZABETH COUCH Ketch	55.5ft. x 17.2 x 7.5
Built: Ramsgate, 1876	Signal Hoist: None	18.21m. x 5.64 x 2.46
Official Number: 75408		NRT: 38
First Owner:	John R. Sandwell, Ramsgate.	Registered: Ramsgate
Second Owner:	1886, Alfred Henry LANFEAR, Union Street, Ramsgate	
		Registered: Ramsgate
Third Owner:	1905, William B STOKES, Weston-Super-Mare	Registered: Bideford
Fourth Owner	1912 James WATTS, Braunton	Registered: Bideford
Fifth Owner:	1913, Thomas WATTS, Selbourne Villas, Braunton	
		Registered: Barnstaple

The vessel foundered off Nash Point, Glamorgan bound from Braunton to Penarth with a cargo of gravel on 22 February 1913. In 1914 A Silver Medal was awarded to Barry Pilot Apprentice Daniel P Davies for rescuing the two man crew from the wreck of the "ELIZABETH COUCH" as she sank.

	ELSIE 3-masted schooner	104.6ft. x 25.0 x 10.1
Built: R. Müller, Faaburg, Denmark, 1876	Signal Hoist: LGSH	31.88m. x 7.62 x 3.08
Official Number 96593		NRT: 137
	Built as the THUSNELDA	
First British Owner:	1895, Christopher Rowbothom, London	Registered: London
Second Owner:	1905, R. C. Roberts, Manchester	Registered: London
Third Owner:	1908, Coppack Bros & Co., Connahs Quay	Registered: London
Fourth Owner:	1909, Tom Coppack & Co., Connahs Quay	Registered: London
Fifth Owner:	1916, W. A. Jenkins, Swansea	Registered: London
Sixth Owner:	1920, Stephen Chugg, Braunton	Registered: London

Previously Danish owned and purchased as a 'mistake', it was suggested she was not properly chocked when built and the vessel leaked abominably. Bearing in mind she had sailed successfully since 1876, she was probably totally worn out when purchased by Steve Chugg, and was quickly scrapped at Velator 1922/25.

190. The remains of the "Elsie" broken up at Velator in the 1920s
Braunton Museum

Built: Duddon Shipbuilding Co. **EMILY BARRATT** ketch 76.8ft. x 20.0 x 8.3
Barrow, 1913   Signal Hoist: MJKD   25.20m. x 6.56 x 2.72
Official Number: 125907   NRT: 51
First Owner: Solomon P. WILSON, Hodbarrow, Millom   Registered: Barrow
Second Owner: 1933, Thomas WELCH, Edith WELCH, Eva A WELCH, and
           John CLARKE of Brau nton   Registered: Barnstaple
                    Sold out of trade, 1959

She subsequently survived into the 1960s and beyond as various roles were thought of for her, including that of a museum ship/display.

191. The "Emily Barratt" at Ilfracombe, 1938
Hugh Thomas

192. "Emily Barrett" entering the refurbished Sea Lock at the entrance to Bude in 1960 - Peter Herbert

Built: William Westacott   **EMMA LOUISE** Ketch   75.4ft. x 19.8 x 8.3
       Barnstaple, 1883.   **Signal Hoist:** None   24.74m. x 6.50 x 2.72
         Official Number: 84475   The last wood vessel built by Westacotts   **NRT:** 66
First Owner: 1883-1900 Francis DRAKE (mgr) 43/64, and
                         Samuel BERRY 21/64, Braunton   **Registered:** Barnstaple
5. 1.1902   At the height Of a severe WNW storm causing exceptionally heavy seas, distress signals were seen coming from the schooners EMMA LOUISE and ELIZABETH MILLER, both from Wick, at anchor in Thurso Bay. The crews of both vessels, 7 men in all were rescued by Thurso lifeboat CO-OPERATOR No. 3. In the severe gale, the lifeboat's mizzen mast was carried away and her fore-mast sprung.
Second Owner: 1906, John L. HARRIS, Alpha Place, Appledore
                                                         Registered: Barnstaple
Third Owner: 1911, John H. GORVIN, Bude Street, Appledore
                                                         Registered: Barnstaple
Fourth Owner: 1926, Rawle Bros, Minehead   **Registered:** Barnstaple
                           Hulked, 1953

193. "Emma Louise" showing the deck layout of an auxiliary ketch of the 1920s.
Braunton Museum

194. Loaded down to her marks the "Emma Louise" delivers another cargo.
Mark Myers

195. "Emma Louise" lying at Appledore in 1953 – Peter Herbert

Built: J. & W. Francis	**ENID** Ketch	61.4ft. x 18.1 x 7.1
Castle Pill, Milford Haven,	Signal Hoist: None	20.14m. x 5.94 x 2.33
Official Number: 108435		NRT: 30

First Owner: David MORGAN, Minfor, Aberayron   Registered: Milford
Second Owner: 1904, O LEWIS   Registered: Cardigan
Third Owner: 1906, Daniel MORGAN, Minfor, Aberayron Registered: Cardigan
Fourth Owner: 1912, Henry H. LLEWHELLI, Broad Haven, Pembroke
                                                                                        Registered: Cardigan
Fifth Owner: 1913-35, Henry S. G. CLARKE (mgr), Fred INCLEDON, and
                       George G. CLARKE   Registered: Barnstaple
Sixth Owner: W. CHICHESTER, Roland CHICHESTER, Braunton
                                                                                        Registered: Barnstaple
Seventh Owner: Sold for trading in the West Indies in 1951.
                       She was lost in a hurricane in 1955.

196. "Enid" sailing off the Valley of Rocks, Lynton in 1937, possibly deep laden with gravel.
Ilfracombe Museum

163

197. "Enid" lying at Velator in 1947 –Robert Andrew

198. "Enid" sailing light in the Bristol Channel in 1939, from the ketch "Clara May" – Braunton Museum

199. The "Enid" at Neath, South Wales, unloading a cargo of gravel
Braunton Museum

200. The ketch "Enid" at Velator Quay – Bill Mitchell

Built: Richard Hill   **F.A.M.E.** Ketch   56.3ft. x 17.9 x 7.8
    Plymouth, 1880   Signal Hoist: VLKF   18.47m. x 5.87 x 2.56
    Official Number: 81044   NRT: 45

Named after the daughters of the builder: Fanny, Anna, Maria and Elizabeth
First Owner: Richard Hill   Registered: Plymouth
Second Owner: 1882, George VICARY, Boutport Street, Barnstaple
    Registered: Plymouth
Third Owner: 1888, George VICARY, Boutport Street, Barnstaple
    Registered: Barnstaple
Owners, Vicary Stribling sold 32/64 to Bernard Tucker and the balance to his wife in 1905.
Fourth Owner: 1905, Bernard TUCKER (mgr), and
    Emma Jane TUCKER, Braunton   Registered: Barnstaple
Lost off the Morte Stone May, 1929. The crew were rescued by the locally owned ketch LEWISMAN.

201. The ketch "F.A.M.E." in Gloucester Docks from a postcard illustration held in Appledore Museum

*202. "F.A.M.E." lying under Lantern Hill, Ilfracombe at low water –
Ilfracombe Museum*

Built: **FAME**   Sloop
                           Signal Hoist: None

Official Number: None   NRT: 36
The vessel was transferred to Ilfracombe 1878, with the master shown as
CHISWELL of Braunton, but we know nothing else.

Built: J. & W. Frances   **FISHGUARD LASS**   Smack   56.8ft. x 16.6 x 6.8
        Milford Haven, 1868   Signal Hoist: None   18.63m. x 5.45 x 2.23
        Official Number: 62792   NRT: 34
First Owner: GWYNNE & Co., Fishguard   Registered: Fishguard
Second Owner: 1884, William PRYTHERCH, Mynythe, Llangian.
                                                                Registered: Carnarvon
Third Owner: 1891, John EVANS, Gegin, Abererch, Pwllheli
                                                                Registered: Carnarvon
Fourth Owner: 1898, George CHUGG, Braunton Converted to Ketch rig
                                                                Registered: Barnstaple
                        Foundered in the Bristol Channel, 1908

Built: Thompson   **FOUR BROTHERS** 2m.schooner   83.8ft. x 20.4 x 9.3
    Northwich, Cheshire, 1877 Signal Hoist: None   27.49m. x 6.69 x 3.05
    Official Number: 67162   NRT: 83
First Owner: Thomas ANDERSON, Brockley Street, Runcorn   Registered: Runcorn
                                                                     1891 NRT reduced to 74
Second Owner: 1906, Arthur Anderson, Leinster Gardens, Runcorn
                                                                           Registered: Runcorn
Third Owner: 1916, William CORNEY, Frederick CORNEY
                and Mary Julia CORNEY   Registered: Barnstaple
              Auxiliary engine fitted 1918
Not listed in Mercantile Navy List 1920, but she foundered off the Orme Head, 1923

See illustration in colour section

Built: **FRIENDS**   Sloop   35.0ft.
    1826   Signal Hoist: None   11.48m.
First Owner:
Second Owner: 1849, John CHUGG, Braunton   Registered: Barnstaple

Built: James Goss   **GARLANDSTONE** Ketch 76.0ft. x 20.2 x 9.0
    Calstock, 1909   Signal Hoist: None   24.93m. x 6.63 x 2.95
    Official Number: 128746   NRT: 62
Laid down in 1904 she was built on speculation and was the largest vessel built by Goss. Named after a rock off Skomer, Pembroke
First Owner: John Davies RUSSAN   Registered: Milford
1912, 40hp. Auxiliary motor installed   NRT: 54
Second Owner: 1919, Andrew MURDOCH, Gloucester.   Registered: Milford
Third Owner: 1943, Alfred PARKHOUSE, Braunton   Registered: Milford
1945 More powerful auxiliary engine installed.
Fourth Owner: 1945 John NEWCOMBE 32/64 and Alfred PARKHOUSE 32/64.
Fifth Owner: 1958 Sold for use as a museum ship at Barmouth, and her Registry
                 was closed.
Sixth Owner: R. A. KYFFIN and Colin LANSDOWN of Porthmadog and taken to Porthmadog as museum ship. The local slate museum became the Gwynedd Maritime Museum and was later absorbed into the National Museum of Wales who chartered the vessel to Morwhelham Quay Trust for display on the River Tamar for 42 years. She was taken there in 1987 where she was restored and is still to be seen at Morwhelham Quay.

203. James Goss' Yard at Calstock in 1909 with "Garlandstone" in frame with the Calstock Viaduct being built.
                         Mark Myers

204. The completed "Garlandstone" ready for launching at Calstock. Nine shipyard workers, including James Goss, can be seen beneath the bows to the right of the picture, and the usual conglomeration of trestles and timber litters the foreground. - Braunton Museum

205. 1909 - At the end of her maiden passage "Garlandstone" lies proudly off her owner master's home at Musselwick, St. Ishmaels in Dale Roads.   Tom Welch

206. "Garlandstone" working out of Swansea – Ilfracombe Museum

Built: **GRACE & ANN** k/k 49ft.8½ins.
1824 Signal Hoist: None 16.29m.
Official Number: None NRT: 59
Owner: 1827, Thomas DARRACOTT, (master), Braunton Registered: Barnstaple

Built: Patje & Zoom **HANNA** Ketch 91.3ft. x 21.1 x 7.8
Waterhuizen, Holland Signal Hoist: None 29.95m. x 6.92 x 2.
NRT: 81
Owners: 1918, George P. HARTNOLL (mgr), Arthur WATTS, Braunton
Registered: Poole
Wrecked off Corbiére, Jersey, 1949

207. The "Hanna" at St. Peter Port, Guernsey, laden with lime in 1948 – Bill Mitchell

208. The "Hanna" arriving at Dunball on the river Parrett in 1947 – Mark Myers

209. The "Hanna" wrecked at La Corbiére, Jersey in 1949 – Bill Mitchell

171

Built: **HAPPY RETURN** Sloop   45ft.2ins
   1800   Signal Hoist: None   14.81m.
Owner: Braunton Owners from 1841   Registered: Barnstaple
Owner Ilfracombe Owners from 1848

Built: **HARRIET** Smack   40.4ft. x 14.0 x 7.1
    Swansea, 1830   Signal Hoist: None   13.25m. x 4.59 x 2.33
    Official Number: 15306   NRT: 22
Owner: 1867, Walter CHICHESTER, Heanton   Registered: Barnstaple
On 7 August 1880, under Captain J. Hancock with a crew of two, and on a voyage from Swansea to Hayle with coal the ship was stranded and totally lost 1½ miles north of Newquay.

Built: Williams   **HEATHERBELL** Ketch   68.4ft. 17.9 x 7.6
    Cardigan, 1873   Signal Hoist: KRSD   22.44m. x 5.87 x 2.49
    Official Number: 63370   NRT: 45
First Owner: To 1884, Thomas DAVIES, Lloyds Wharf, Cardigan
                                                   Registered: Cardigan
Second Owner: To 1888, Richard THOMAS, Hendre Villas, Barmouth
                                                   Registered: Cardigan
Third Owner: 1889-91, Fraser Ede BUNT, Tintagel   Registered: Padstow
Fourth Owner: 1906, Joseph KNIGHT, The Docks, Lydney
                                                   Registered: Barnstaple
Fifth Owner: 1912, George CLARKE, Wrafton 22/64   Registered: Barnstaple
         and Thomas CLARKE, 42/64, Braunton
             Dr. ELISTON-WRIGHT of Braunton was also said to have had an interest in this vessel.
             Stranded South Dogger Bank, Wexford, 1916

Built: **HELSTONE**   Smack   63.4ft. 18.7 x 10.4
    Fowey, 1831   Signal Hoist: MFHL   20.80m. x 6.13 x 3,41
    Official Number: 17107   NRT: 59
First Owner: SPERSHOTT & Co.   Registered: Falmouth
             Used as a packet vessel London to Falmouth
Owner: 1883, James WATTS, Braunton. Refitted as a ketch   Registered: Barnstaple
             Sold for breaking up 1897

Built: **HENRIETTA** Schooner   76.0ft.
    Prince Edward Island, 1859 Signal Hoist: SBKH 24.93m.
    Official Number: 36815   NRT: 68
1864, Registry transferred from Newport to Barnstaple, owned in Braunton
Later sold to Appledore owners and from there to Ireland
Owner: 1884, Michael KENEFIK, Crosshaven, Co. Cork   Registered: Cork

Built: Hinks at Appledore **HILDA** Smack/barge   30ft.
    Circa 1920   9.842m.
First Owner: Harry 'Blue' Mitchell, South Street, Braunton   Registered: n/a
Built without an engine she was one of the last sailing gravel barges constructed and, working "inside" the Bar she was not registered with the Board of Trade, and

did not carry an official number. At some time an auxiliary motor was installed. Sold in the 1950s to a Welsh family for use as a pleasure vessel, on her first passage under the new owners, in attempting to cross the Bar, two crew members were swept off the bow of the vessel and drowned. The vessel survived and returned to Braunton.

210. The gravel barge "Hilda", the last such vessel to work under sail, with Harry 'Blue' Mitchell and his two daughters.- Photo courtesy Tom Welch

211. The little gravel barge "Hilda," light before proceeding to the loading area off Crow Point. - Braunton Museum

Built: Messeroy   **HONOUR** Cutter   57.1ft. x 16.2 x .7.5
    Jersey, 1862   Signal Hoist: None   18.73m. x 5.31 x 2.46
    Official Number: 45275   NRT: 36
First Owner: HAMON & Co., St. Helier.   Registered: Jersey
Second Owner: 1884-91, Lewis J GAUVRY, 71, Travel Street, Plymouth
    Registered: Jersey
    Rigged as a Ketch   NRT: 31
Third Owner: 1906, Robert PICKETT, 71, Fore Street, Ilfracombe
    Registered: Jersey
Understood to have been owned for a short period by S. MITCHELL and T. BUTLER of Braunton
    Not listed in Mercantile Navy List 1912

Built: **HOPE** Brigantine   49ft.6ins.
    1801   Signal Hoist: None   16.24m.
    Official Number: NRT: 46
Owned 1875, Braunton   Registered: Bideford

Built: **HOPE** 2m. Schooner   50.0ft. x 15.5 x 9.0
    1803   Signal Hoist: None   16.5m. x 5.08 x 2.95
    Official Number: 15536   NRT: 42
Registry transferred to Barnstaple 1851
Owner: 1862, Thomas DARRACOTT, Braunton   Registered: Barnstaple

Built: **HOPE** Smack   40.9ft. x 14.1 x 6.3
    Undy, Monmouth, 1837   Signal Hoist: KQLS   13.42m. 4.62 x 2.07
    Official Number: 10917   NRT: 20
Registry transferred to Barnstaple 1857
Owner: 1867, Thomas WHITE, Braunton 64/54   Registered: Barnstaple
Owned: 1884-89, Lewellin TWINNING, Bristol   Registered: Barnstaple
    No longer in Mercantile Navy List, 1891.

Built: Robert Johnson   **I'LL TRY** Smack   67ft. x 17.25 x 8.85
    Bideford, 1853   Signal Hoist: None   21.98m. x 5.66 x 2.90
    Official Number: 1432   NRT: 56
First Owner: Robert Johnson, Bideford   Registered: Bideford
Second Owner: 1888, Eliza LEMON, Barnstaple. 64/64 Rigged as a Ketch
    Registered: Barnstaple
Third Owner: 1890, William HARRIS (Lime Burner) Velator. 64/64
    Registered: Barnstaple
    Converted to a coal hulk, 1893

Built: **DESMOND** Ketch   77ft. x 17.6 x 7.1
   Bideford, 1864   Signal Hoist: None   25.26m. x 5.77 x 2.33
   Official Number: 91067   NRT: 43
No information shown prior to 1889.
Owner: 1889, Arthur Benjamin PERRY, 127, Redcliff Street, Bristol
                                                      Registered: Bristol

Lengthened 1891 at Cleave Houses, Bideford
                    Renamed **IRON KING**
Owner: 1891-1906, John MOSS, Clovelly   Registered: Bideford
Bottom rebuilt 1899
She is believed to have been owned between 1910-1912 by James WATTS of Braunton
Owner: 1912-1920, William M. ACKFORD, 36, New Street, Appledore
                                                     Registered: Bideford

                    Renamed **SALTASH**
Owner: 1934, JEFFORD & SONS Ltd, Burraton Combe, Saltash
                                                     Registered: Plymouth

Built: P. Hancock   **ISABEL** Ketch   63ft. x 18.1x 6.9
   Milford, 1897   Signal Hoist: SFCH   20.67m.x 5.94 x 2.26
   Official Number: 108427   NRT: 42
First Owner: to 1910, John JAMES, Grey House, St. Dogmaels
                                                       Registered: Milford
Second Owner: 1912, James JAMES, Grey House, St. Dogmaels
                                                      Registered: Milford
Third Owner: 1913, William N. GEORGE, Rosebush, Pembroke
                                                      Registered: Milford
Fourth Owner: 1914, James WATTS and A. CORNEY, Braunton
                                                    Registered: Barnstaple
Fifth Owner: 1918, Mrs. Jamesina CARTER, Tower Park, Fowey
                                                    Registered: Fowey
                                                    NRT: 40
Sixth Owner: 1934, Alfred W. POOLEY, Harbour Road, Par Registered: Fowey

212. "Isabel" proceeding to sea.
Peter Welch

Built: Thomas Waters	**J.M.J.** Ketch	75.4ft. x 19.5 x 9.6
Bideford, 1867	Signal Hoist: JHNS	24.74m. x 6.40 x 3.15
Official Number: 56030		NRT: 60

First Owner: John M. JONES, Swansea Registered: Swansea

The vessel was named after John, Mary and James Jones, but was always known as *"Jam, Marmalade, Jelly"*

Second Owner: 1870, John Jones, Port Talbot Registered: Pt. Talbot

Third Owner: 1883-91, John THOMAS, Daniel Street, Newport
  Registered: Newport

Third Owner: 1891, Charles HUNT, 48/64, and Mary Alice CLARKE
  16/64, of Braunton Registered: Barnstaple

Fourth Owner: 1897, Charles HUNT 64/64 of Braunton Registered: Barnstaple

She was on a regular run with pipe clay from Bideford to Glasgow, returning with around 100/125 tons of coal to Combe Martin.

Lost on 15 August 1903 on Iron Rock off the coast of the Isle of Arran in the Firth of Clyde on passage from Bideford to Glasgow with a cargo of pipe clay, under Captain Charles Hunt, carrying a crew of 3 with 2 passengers, when she was stranded and lost in wind conditions NNW Force 1. The master would not leave the vessel but two boys got the boat out and tried to scull it from under the bow, but the boat drove against the bows and capsized. The boys gained the beach and climbed the cliffs to alert the local farmer, Mr. Hamilton.

She was a sister ship to the "H.F. BOLT."

213. The ketch "J.M.J." wrecked on the Isle of Arran – Braunton Museum

Built: Massey   **J.M.P.** Ketch   63.2ft. x 18.3 x 7.6
    Portreath, 1874   Signal Hoist: None   20.73m. x 6.0 x 2.49
    Official Number: 68862   NRT: 36
Owner: 1916, H. S. G. CLARKE, Dr. Elliston WRIGHT,   Registered: Barnstaple
    Grace Ann INCLEDON and Mary Alice CLARKE
    Stranded west of Ilfracombe in 1917, and became a total loss.

Built: T. Bennett   **JANE & SARAH** Smack 60.2ft. x 17.0 x 7.9
    Padstow, 1855   Signal Hoist: LVSR   19.75m. x 5.58 x 2.59
    Official Number: 16048   NRT: 44
First Owner: BRENTON & Co   Registered: Padstow
Second Owner: 1859, E. HUGHES, Holyhead   Registered: Holyhead
Third Owner: 1884-89, Rowland OWEN, Caeia, Llaneilgo, Anglesey
     Registered: Beaumaris
Fourth Owner: 1890, Sarah WEBBER, Vicarage Lawn, Barnstaple
     Registered: Barnstaple
Fifth Owner: 1905, Phillip K. HARRIS, Appledore   Registered: Barnstaple
Sixth Owner: 1906, Robert DRAKE, Wrafton 64/64   Registered: Barnstaple
Seventh Owner: 1907, John AYRE, Braunton, 64/64   Registered, Barnstaple
Eighth Owner: 1912, Mrs. Henrietta AYRE, Wrafton, Braunton
     Registered: Barnstaple
Ninth Owner: 1919, Beatrice E. HUTCHINGS, Irsha Street, Appledore
     Registered: Barnstaple
Ninth Owner: 1924, Jack MITCHELL 32/64 Frank MITCHELL 32/64
    of Braunton   Registered: Barnstaple
    Broken up at Velator 1928

Built: William Westacott   **JOHN & ANN** Smack   49.5ft. x 14.4 x 7.2
    Barnstaple, 1840   Signal Hoist: LRVK   16.24m. x 4.72 x 2.36
    Official Number: 15338   NRT: 38
First Owner: WERSFOLD   Registered: Barnstaple
Second Owner: 1870, Henry DRAKE, Braunton   Registered: Barnstaple
    1895: Re-rigged as a Ketch for the same owner.
    Broken up in the early 1900s.

Built: Scoble & Davies   **JULIE** Ketch   57.6ft. x 17.6 x 6.5
    Malpas, Truro, 1889   Signal Hoist: JGWQ   18.89m. x 5.77 x 2.13
    Official Number: 84514   NRT: 38½
Built principally of teak taken from old men-of-war being broken up at Devonport and Falmouth.
First Owner: Peter HUNKIN, Mevagissey   Registered: Truro
Second Owner: 1902, John Squire CHICHESTER, East St, Braunton
     Registered: Barnstaple
Third Owner: 1912-14, NOBEL EXPLOSIVE Co. Ltd, Glasgow
     Registered: Barnstaple
Fourth Owner: 1920, David DAVIES, Mount Stewart Square, Cardiff
     Registered: Barnstaple
Fifth Owner: 1930, Banning VOYSEY, 9, Ferry Road, Topsham
     Registered: Barnstaple

Sixth Owner: 1934, William R. VOYSEY, Shapter Street, Topsham
Registered: Barnstaple
Dismasted and sunk off the Eddystone 29 January 1935 without loss of life.

214. The "Julie" when owned in Topsham sailing on the Exe Estuary – Mark Myers

Built: William White   **KATE** 2-masted schooner   82.8ft. x 20.8 x 9.7
        Canal Side, Ulverston,   Signal Hoist: None   27.16m. x 6,82 x 3,18
        Barrow, 1874   NRT: 86
        Official Number: 70473

First Owner: To 1906, William POSTLETHWAITE, Holborn Hill   Registered: Barrow
Second Owner: 1911-1920, Lewis ALDRIDGE, Arlingham, Gloucs.
Registered: Barrow
Third Owner: 1924, Hugh SHAW and William SHAW   Registered: Barrow

Captain Hugh Shaw who commanded the vessel from 1911, tells of surviving an Irish Sea gale at Christmas, 1912, that caused the loss of the *Harvest Queen*. He stayed with the *Kate* throughout the First World War, employing her in the cross-channel trade and surviving an encounter with a U-boat in 1918. In 1920 he had an engine fitted to the schooner, and then in 1922 he left the *Kate* under his brother, Capt. William Shaw. Captain Hugh Shaw and his father-in-law Lewis Aldridge were the shareholders, the Shaw family selling the vessel in 1928 to a group of Braunton owners.

Fourth Owner: 1934, Harry C. CHUGG, Station Road, Braunton
Registered: Barrow
She is believed to have broken her back about 1935, whilst lying at Barnstaple

215. The "Kate", rigged as a ketch, lying at Ilfracombe with small smack alongside.
Ilfracombe Museum

216. The topsail schooner "Kate" under full sail as she was originally rigged
Mark Myers

Built: **KITTY ANN** Brigantine 62.0ft. x 18.3 x 8.5
    Appledore, 1856   Signal Hoist: LRWF   20.34m. x 6.00 x 2.79
    Official Number 15349   NRT: 56
First Owner: John CHUGG, Braunton   Registered: Barnstaple
     Re-rigged as a schooner and later as a ketch.
Second Owner: 1873, John CHUGG, Wrafton   Registered: Barnstaple
Third Owner: 1884-1914, George CHUGG, Braunton   Registered: Barnstaple
                                                           NRT: 49
Fourth Owner: 1917, Harry CHUGG, Ernest CHUGG,   Registered: Barnstaple
     George CHUGG and Hilda CHUGG all of Braunton
By 1920 she was no longer listed in the Mercantile Navy List and was broken up in 1925 having remained in the same family for some 70 years.

217. The "Kitty Ann" (left) and the "Yeo", (see later), on the gravel banks.
Len Baglole

218. The crew of the "Kitty Ann" and the gang of loaders pose under the bows, whilst loading a cargo of gravel from the banks. Their names are left to right, standing: Captain E. Chugg, R. Bray, M. Butson, T. Bassett, F. Mock and W. Williams; and seated on the maunds – or loading baskets - L. Cousins, J. Slee and, with the dog, Tom Watts. – Braunton Museum

219. The "Kitty Ann" (front) and the "Mary" being broken up at Velator about 1925
Braunton Museum

Built: Aubin   **LADY OF THE ISLES** Dandy   60.1ft. x 16.8 x 7.9
    Jersey, 1868   Signal Hoist: KCDQ   19.72m. x 5.51 x 2.59
    Official Number: 55302   NRT: 44
First Owner: PAYNE & Co.   Registered: Jersey
Second Owner: 1871, John HOLMAN   Registered: Guernsey
Third Owner: 1880-1891, Harry Harry L READ, Saundersfoot Registered: Guernsey
Fourth Owner: 1906-1935, John DAVIES, Lindy Villa, Saundersfoot
     Registered: Milford
     1934 Signal Hoist altered to : MJRK
Fifth Owner: 1936, Jack WATTS, Braunton   Registered: Milford
Later understood to be owned by J. IRWIN of Combe Martin.

Built: **LARK** Ketch   52.5ft. x 17.0 x 7.5
    Bridgwater, 1856   Signal Hoist: KQNC   17.22m. x 5.58 x 2.46
    Official Number: 10937   NRT: 36
First Owner: 1856-65, H. LEIGH, Bridgwater   Registered: Bridgwater
Owner: 1884, Richard JONES, Portmadoc   Registered: Cardiff
Owner: 1886-90, Catherine JONES, Bryn Golen, Penrhyndeudraeth
     Registered: Cardiff
Owner: Tom BASSETT, John CHICHESTER, East Street, Braunton
     Registered: Cardiff
     1891 – not listed

220. The ketch "Lark" at Pilton – Tom Welch

221. Captain Thomas Gideon Bassett (left) and his crew of two aboard the ketch "Lark". The boy can be seen to the rear. Thomas Bassett was later the pilot for vessels traversing Braunton Pill.
Tom Welch

Built: E. T. Bennett	**LENORA** Ketch	50.8ft. x 15.3 x 7.3
Padstow, 1854	Signal Hoist: MRCP	16.66m. x 5.02 x 2.39
Official Number: 19225		NRT: 38

First Owner: 1854-1870, HUTCHINGS, Padstow — Registered: Padstow
Owner: 1884, Walter CHICHESTER, Braunton — Registered: Padstow
Owner: 1885, Walter CHICHESTER, Braunton — Registered: Barnstaple
Owner: 1901-12, Mary Jane CHICHESTER (widow), Braunton Registered: Barnstaple
Owner: 1902, William Henry CHICHESTER, Braunton had shares

Wrecked on 19 November 1913 when, following collision with the tug ATLAS of Barrow-in-Furness, she was driven ashore near the Mumbles in Swansea Bay to prevent her sinking. Bad weather prevented salvage and she became a total loss. At the time she was on passage from Cardiff to Bideford with coal and culm and a crew of three.

Built:	**LEWISMAN** Schooner	90.1ft. x 18.1 x 8.1
Stornaway, 1878	Signal Hoist: None	29.56m. x 5.94 x 2.66
Official Number: 79131		NRT: 58

First Owner: Donald ROSS, Invergordon, Ross-shire — Registered: Stornaway
Second Owner: 1884-1891, William H. SARAH, Woolster St, Plymouth
                                                                          Registered: Stornaway
                    1889, Converted to Ketch rig
Third Owner: 1895, William HOLDEN, Oreston, Plymouth Registered: Stornaway
Fourth Owner: 1901, William Kingdon SLADE, Irsha St, Appledore
                                                                          Registered: Bideford

Fifth Owner: 1912, James SLADE, Westcroft Terrace, Appledore
Registered: Bideford
1927, Auxiliary engine fitted.
Sixth Owner: 1927, Sidney W. SLATTER, Brunswick Wharf, Barnstaple
Registered: Bideford

The connection with Braunton is the ownership of shares by MITCHELL of Braunton at the period of SLATTER'S managing ownership until she was sold on in 1946.

Seventh Owner: 1946, Scottish owners   Registered: Leith
Broken up at Granton, 1949

222. "Lewisman" lying in Braunton Pill – Peter Herbert

223. The ketches "Lewisman" (left), "Ann" and "C.F.H." - Braunton Museum

224. "Lewisman" at Gould's Store, Barnstaple. – Braunton Museum

Built:	**LIBERTY** Smack	59.6ft. x 16.0 x 9.0
Haverfordwest, 1795	Signal Hoist: MRNC	19.55m. x 5.25 x 2.95
Official Number: 19337		NRT: 55

Owner: 1851-1865, ANDREWS   Registered: St. Ives
1851, Lengthened, new deck and large repairs. Re-rigged as a 2-masted schooner.
Owner: 1865-1885, Robert MORTON, Terrace, St. Ives   Registered: St. Ives
Owner: 1886-1891, William OLDHAM, Padstow   Registered: St. Ives
Owner: 1892, James WATTS, Braunton, 64/64   Registered: Barnstaple
                       Broken up 1898

Built	**LILLY** Sloop	41ft.6ins
1830	Signal Hoist: None	13.61m
Official Number: Not known		NRT: 23

    Understood to have been owned in Braunton. Broken up at Bickington, 1860.

Built: Burt	**LINDA** Ketch	57.3ft. 17.1 x 7.6
Falmouth, 1878	Signal Hoist: SNGT	18.80m. x 5.61 x 2.49
Official Number: 78190		NRT: 34

First Owner: Norman GREY, Penryn, Cornwall   Registered: Falmouth
Second Owner: 1888, Francis DRAKE and William DRAKE, Braunton
                                                   Registered: Barnstaple

Third Owner: 1889, Francis DRAKE (jr.) 32/64, Samuel BERRY 32/64
Registered: Barnstaple
Fourth Owner: 1891, William DRAKE, Braunton   Registered: Barnstaple

On 29 January 1900 whilst on passage from Lydney to Barnstaple with coal with a crew of two, she foundered in Barnstaple Bay, off Hartland following a collision with the schooner SARAH & JANE, which lost her bowsprit.

Built: F. J. Carver   **MAGGIE ANNIE** Ketch   76.5ft. x 20.2 x 9.0
    Bridgwater, 1881   Signal Hoist: WGFV   25.10m. x 6.63 x 2.95
    Official Number: 78706   NRT: 69
First Owner: Richard HILLMAN, Epney, Gloucester   Registered: Gloucester
Second Owner: 1899, William DRAKE, Braunton, 64/64   Registered: Barnstaple
Third Owner: 1912, William CORNEY, Wrafton   Registered: Barnstaple
Fourth Owner: 1920, Alfred William CORNEY, 16/64, Frank CORNEY 16/64
    Frederick C. CORNEY, 32/64, Braunton   Registered: Barnstaple
Fifth Owner: 1932, Kimberley G. FOSTER, Tideford, St. Germans
    Registered: Barnstaple

Broken up 1947

225. The "Maggie Annie" lying off Appledore
    Appledore Museum

BuilT: W. Shilston   **MARGARET** Ketch   68.8ft. x 18.4 x 7.0
        Plymouth, 1903   Signal Hoist: None   22.57m. x 6.04 x 2.30
        Official Number: 105244   NRT: 42
First Owner: John Lamey, Ship Inn, New Quay, Appledore   Registered: Bideford
Second Owner: 1912-14, Ellen A. LAMEY, Ship Inn, Appledore Registered: Bideford
                    Not listed in Mercantile Navy List 1920

226. *A group of ketches lying in Bude in the early 1900s. The vessel carrying the white sail is the "Margaret" – Appledore Museum*

227. *"Margaret" leaving Appledore.*
M. Cann Collection, Appledore Museum

Built: J. & W. Francis   **MARJORIE** Ketch   78.8ft. x 20.3 x 9.3
   Castle Pill, Pembroke Dock   Signal Hoist: None   25.85m. x 6.66 x 3.05
   Milford Haven   NRT: 74
   Official Number: 112466
First Owner: William FRANCIS, Castle Pill, Milford Haven   Registered: Milford
Second Owner: 1910, William DRAKE, Braunton 64/64   Registered: Barnstaple
Auxiliary engine fitted 1916
        Believed to have been sunk by U-boat, 1917

Built: **MARY** Sloop   39ft. x 14.0 x 7.0
   1795   Signal Hoist: None   12.79m. x 4.59 x 2.30
     Official Number: None   NRT: 29
Owner: 1827, J. L. HAYDON, Braunton   Registered: Barnstaple
          Foundered in Bristol Channel, 1856

Built: **MARY** Ketch
   Bridgwater, Date of build not known   Signal Hoist: None
     Official Number: 18967   NRT: 26
Owner: 1884-1914, William Thomas GIBBS, Bridgwater   Registered: Bridgwater
Owner: 1920, Mary A. GIBBS, Chilton Road, Bridgwater   Registered: Bridgwater
This vessel is said to have been owned by E. J. PEDDER of Lynmouth, with John Squire CHICHESTER of Braunton as master, and this may have been in the later 1920s.
              Not listed 1934

Built: **MARY ANN** Brigantine 51ft.
  1818   Signal Hoist: None   16.73m.
  Official Number: None   NRT: 49
Owned in Braunton in 1841, but no other details

Built: C. Luhring   **MARY ELIEZER** Ketch   81.6ft. x 18.0 x 7.7
  Hammilwarder, Germany, 1904   Signal Hoist: HBMQ   26.77m. 5,90 x 2,53
  Official Number: 118818   NRT: 58
First Owner: 1904-1914 James GLEADHILL, Mary's Place, Barton-on-Humber
                                                           Registered: Hull
Second Owner: 1917, George CLARKE, 7, Hills View, Braunton   Registered: Hull
Requisitioned by the Admiralty for service with the Royal Navy during World War II,
            she was sold to Danish owners in 1947.

228. The "Mary Eliezer" discharging in Newport, Isle of Wight circa 1940 – Bill Cook

229. The graceful lines of the "Mary Eliezer" seen to advantage in Ilfracombe. Bill Cook

189

230. *The "Mary Eliezer" and a steamship seen together in the Richmond Dry Dock at Appledore – Bill Cook*

Built: Thomas Geen   **MARY GRACE** Ketch   56.6ft. x 16.5 x 7.0
    Appledore, 1852   Signal Hoist: None   18.57m. x 5.41 x 2.30
    Official Number: 15323   NRT: 52
First Owner: John CHUGG, Braunton   Registered: Barnstaple
Second Owner: 1884-1891, George G. CLARKE, Heanton Funchardon, Braunton
                                                                Registered: Barnstaple
Owner: 1891-1914, William CORNEY, Wrafton, Braunton with John CHUGG,
     Alfred CORNEY and H.S.G.CLARKE of Braunton   Registered: Barnstaple
                             Refitted 1917
Owner: 1922 Philip K. HARRIS, Appledore   Registered: Barnstaple
Note: Not listed in Mercantile Navy List after 1920
                             Broken up 1926

Built: Black   **MARY STEWART** 2-m Schooner   72.5ft. x 19.5 x 8.3
       Montrose, Scotland, 1876   Signal Hoist: None   23.79m. x 6.40 x 2.72
       Official Number: 72414   Built of iron.   NRT: 59
First Owner: James STEWART, Strone, Aygyle (to 1886)   Registered: Greenock
Second Owner: 1906, William WEAVER, Isle of Whitehorn, Wigtown
                                                                    Registered: Greenock
Third Owner: 1912, George H MEADOWS, Francis Villa, Epney, Gloucester
                                                                    Registered: Greenock
Fourth Owner: 1925-58, Florence E. PARKHOUSE, Barton Lane, Braunton
                         Captain W. PARKHOUSE   Registered. Greenock

1939-1945 – was used as a Royal Naval storeship on charter to the Admiralty. She was the last commercial sailing vessel to carry a jib-boom

Fifth Owner: 1958, Percy FERGUSON, St. Peter Port, Guernsey
                                                            Registered: Greenock

Sixth Owner: 1959, Peter HERBERT, Bude   Registered: Greenock

Sold to American owners 1963 for use as a yacht, and arrived in Santander on 3 August 1963, where she was refitted for cruising. At the time of her sale abroad she was the oldest vessel on the British Register.

231. The figurehead of the "Mary Stewart"
Mark Myers

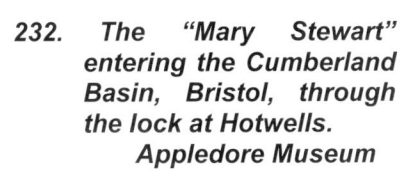

232. The "Mary Stewart" entering the Cumberland Basin, Bristol, through the lock at Hotwells.
Appledore Museum

233. The "Mary Stewart" discharging the last cargo to be unloaded at Velator Quay about 1950. The coal was destined for the bulb farm in Sandy Lane, Braunton.
Braunton Museum

MAUDE Schooner

Built:
   Widnes, 1865   Signal Hoist: None
   Official Number: 62010   NRT: 59

Originally owned in North Wales and used in the slate trade until 1910.
Owner: 1884- 1906, Thomas HUGHES, South Penrallt, Port Dinorwic, Caernarvon
                                                                              Registered: Runcorn
Owner: 1912-1920, Joseph KNIGHT, The Docks, Lydney, Glos. Registered: Bideford
                          Converted to a ketch
                          Engine installed in 1929
After a period laid up at Ilfracombe she resumed trading in the Bristol Channel in 1934
Owner: B. TUCKER and R. PARKER, Braunton   Registered: Bideford
Owner: 1934, Mrs. Doris TUCKER, , North Street, Braunton   Registered: Bideford
                               Broken up 1946

234. "Maude" rigged as a ketch, preparing to leave Appledore – Peter Welch

235. "Maude" alongside Rolle Quay, at Barnstaple.
　　　　　　Braunton Museum

Built:	**MERLIN** Smack	34ft.5ins.
1839	Signal Hoist: None	11.29m.
Official Number: None		NRT: 16
Owner: 1846, in Braunton		Registered: Barnstaple

Built: W. Allsop   **MICHAEL KELLY** Steam Tug   112ft. x 20.1 x 9.9
    Preston, 1871   Signal Hoist: LRKW   36.74m. x 6.59 x 3.25
    Official Number: 45688   Built of iron   NRT: 95
First Owner: Dundalk Harbour Commissioners, Dundalk   Registered: Dundalk
Second Owner: 1890, Ellis Owen ROBERTS, Water Street, Liverpool
    Registered: Liverpool
Converted to a 3-masted schooner with auxiliary 23 n.h.p. 2-cylinder oil engine
Third Owner: 1910, Albert WESTCOTT, Woolster Street, Plymouth
    Registered: Liverpool
    No longer listed Mercantile Navy List after 1920
Fourth Owner: 1926-7, Mrs RYAN and E. DONNELLY   Not registered
The Braunton link is the fact that the vessel was moored for some years at Broad Sands, near White House, Braunton being under Captain C Hunt and the mate, W. Hunt of Braunton. The vessel was probably de-registered 1920 and broken up over a period before 1930.

Built: Duncan   **MORNING STAR** Schooner 117.0ft. x 26.1 x 14.6
    Elgin, Kingston-on-Spey, 1878 Signal Hoist: RMGV   26.97m. 6.57 x 3.14
    Official Number: 70529   NRT: 100
First Owner: James McBEATH, Thurso, Wick   Registered: Wick
Second Owner: 1890-1917, Aaron SLOGGETT, Padstow   Registered: Padstow
Third Owner: 1917-20, Bertie CORNEY, Alfred CORNEY, Lily CORNEY, Frank
    CORNEY, and Alfred AYRE of Braunton   Registered: Barnstaple
Fourth Owner: 1920, Bertie CORNEY, Wrafton   Registered: Barnstaple
Fifth Owner: 1923, Alfred W. CORNEY, Braunton   Registered: Barnstaple
    11 September 1923, on passage with a cargo of bar, sheet and rod steel she foundered off Porlock

236. "Morning Star" of Padstow when rigged as a topsail schooner outside Hawkins coal yard at Padstow about 1900
David B. Clement Collection

237. Captain Alfred Corney (right) and his crew of the "Morning Star" in 1917
Braunton Museum

	MOUSE Ketch	
Built: T. Grendon & Co.		69.6ft. x 16.1 x 7.1
Drogheda, 1878	Signal Hoist: None	22.83m. 5.28 x 2.33
Official Number: 78426		NRT: 48
First Owner: Frederick St. G SMITH, Drogheda		Registered: Drogheda

Second Owner: 1900, The Cardigan Mercantile Co. Ltd, Lancelot LOWTHER
　　　　　　　　　　　　　　　　　　　　　　　　　　　　Registered: Cardigan

Third Owner　1913, William H. STEPHENS, Woolster Street, Plymouth
　　　　　　　　　　　　　　　　　　　　　　　　　　　　Registered: Cardigan

Fourth Owner:　1915, Harry DRAKE, Braunton　　Registered: Cardigan

Lost off Ilfracombe on passage from Swansea with a cargo of basic slag in 1916. She put into Ilfracombe for shelter but demurred at the harbour charges and put to sea again, being overwhelmed off the Morte Stone and sinking with the loss of her Master, Captain Henry DRAKE and one crewmember, Willy Cole, whose bodies were buried at Heanton. The third crew member missed the train for Swansea at Barnstaple, and failing to join the vessel, so survived!

238. The ketch "Mouse" when owned in Cardigan awaiting entry to the port on Teifi Bar.

Built: William Westcott   **NELLIE** Ketch   74.7ft. x 20.6 x 8.8
    Barnstaple, 1874   Signal Hoist: None   24.51m. 6.76 x 2.89
    Official Number: 68200   NRT: 71
Owner: Francis DRAKE, Wrafton   Registered: Barnstaple
The vessel went missing around 7 November 1881 on passage from St. John, Newfoundland to Oporto loaded with salt cod.

Built: J. & W. Harvey,   **NELLIE** Ketch   85.3ft. x 19.1 x 6.8
    Clymping, Littlehampton, 1882 Signal Hoist: WLVQ   27.98m. x 6.27 x 2.23
    Official Number: 81983   NRT: 70
First Owner: John HARVEY, Littlehampton   Registered: Littlehampton
Second Owner: 1918, William K. WATSON, Station Road, Grangemouth
                                                      Registered: Littlehampton
Third Owner: 1921, HUXTABLE, Braunton   Registered: Littlehampton
    Coincidentally this *Nellie* also foundered on passage to Newfoundland

Built: Qualtrough   **OCEAN GEM** Ketch   69.8ft. x 18.7 x 8.0
    Castletown, Isle of Man, 1864   Signal Hoist: MJZN   22.90m. x 6.13 x 2.62
    Official Number: 47281   NRT: 44
Rebuilt 1882 at Port St. Mary, Isle of Man
Owner: 1882-1891, Edward GALE, Castletown, Isle of Man   Registered: Castletown
Owner: 1891-1912, John MILLIGAN, Merklund, Dumfries   Registered: Dumfries
Owner: 1913, Samuel VERNON, Creetown, Kirkcudbright   Registered: Dumfries
Owner: 1920, John FORD, Pemboke Mills, Pembroke   Registered: Dumfries
Owner: 1922, Harry Cecil CHUGG, Church Street, Braunton 64/64
                                                      Registered: Barnstaple
                Broken up at Velator August 1935

239. The "Ocean Gem" at Rolle Quay, Barnstaple in the 1920s. The inside vessel is the "Bessie Clark" - *Braunton Museum*

Built: J. Duncan   **OLIVE BRANCH** Schooner   78.3ft. x 19.5 x 9.9
    Elgin, Kingston-on-Spey, 1878 Signal Hoist: LMCV   25.69m. x 6.40 x 3.25
    Official Number: 76578   NRT: 56
First Owner: 1878-88 John McWILLIAM, High Street, Buckie   Registered: Banff
Second Owner: 1889-96, James PEARCE, Commerce House, Porthcawl
         Registered: Fowey
Third Owner: 1897, Henry Gould CLARKE 32/64 Braunton
      F. H. DALBY 32/64   Registered: Barnstaple
Fourth Owner: 1900, Henry Gould CLARKE 64/64, Braunton   Registered: Barnstaple
Fifth Owner: 1909, Alfred AYRE, 48/64 Braunton   Registered: Barnstaple
      1919, Auxiliary oil engine fitted
Sixth Owner: 1933, Philip K. HARRIS, Appledore, 64/64   Registered: Barnstaple

Build: William Westacott   **ORPHAN GIRL** 2-m Schooner 76ft. x 21.8 x 8.6
    Barnstaple, 1873   Signal Hoist: None   24.93m. x 7.15 x 2.82.
    Official Number: NRT: 87
First Owner: HARDING   Registered: Barnstaple
       Wrecked 1881

Built: H. M. Restarick   **PILOT**   Dandy
    Bideford, 1831   Signal Hoist: LRSJ
    Official Number: 15307   NRT: 29
Owner: 1884-91, Henry STEVENS, Braunton   Registered: Barnstaple
       Converted to ketch
     Not listed Mercantile Navy List 1906

Built: G. & P. Copeland   **PIRATE**   Ketch   59.6ft. x 19.1 x 7.9
    Sromness, 1888   Signal Hoist: None   19.55m. x 6.27 x 2.59
    Official Number: 91454   NRT: 48
First Owner: Peter JOHNSON, Copeland, Stromness   Registered: Kirkwall
Second Owner: 1888, Robert DRAKE, Wrafton, and Francis DRAKE, J. HARTNOLL
     Master T. Coates, all of Braunton   Registered: Barnstaple
Third Owner: 1913, Philip K. HARRIS, Appledore   Registered: Barnstaple
22 November 1913, on passage Cardiff to Bideford with coal she foundered off Lavernock Point following a collision with the ss DRUIDSTONE of Cardiff.

Built: J. White   **PLEIADES**   Ketch   63.9 x 17.1 x 7.1
    Cowes, Isle of Wight, 1877   Signal Hoist: QSTW   20.96m. x 5.61 x 2.33
    Official Number: 74450   NRT: 43
First Owner: Thomas W. RABSEY, West Cowes   Registered: Cowes
Second Owner: 1886, Robert CROUCHER, Quay Street, Newport, Isle of Wight
         Registered: Cowes
Third Owner: 1902, Henry H. DRAKE, Wrafton 64/64   Registered: Barnstaple
Fourth Owner: 1914, Mrs. Eva J. DRAKE, Wrafton   Registered: Barnstaple
1916 - Captain Henry Haache DRAKE died at sea in the wreck of the MOUSE (qv).
Refitted 1925 and converted to a houseboat in the 1950s
     Not listed Mercantile Navy List 1934

240. The ketch "Pleiades" in Minehead Harbour – Bill Mitchell

Built: R. Lewis   **PRIORY** Ketch   58.0ft. x 17.7 x 6.9
     Milford Haven, 1870   Signal Hoist: None   19.03m. x 5.81 x 2.26
     Official Number: 62799   NRT: 38
Owner: 1870, Eliza INCLEDON, Frederick INCLEDON, Grace INCLEDON,
     and Joseph INCLEDON, Francis DRAKE all of Braunton
     Registered: Barnstaple
Owner: 1884-91 Mark BIDDLE, Portishead, Somerset   Registered: Milford
Owner: 1906, Frederick J. INCLEDON, Heanton Road, Braunton
     Registered: Barnstaple
Owner: 1914, Mrs. Grace INCLEDON, Braunton   Registered: Barnstaple
Vessel altered in 1919 but did not appear in Mercantile Navy List after 1920 and may have become a lighter.

Built: **PRUDENCE & ELIZA** Sloop   39ft.10" x 13ft.2" x 6ft.8"
     Swansea, 1819   Signal Hoist: None   13.09m. x 4.29 x 2.18
     Official Number: NRT: 21
Owner: R. K. SYMONDS, merchant of Braunton

Built: Thomas Waters   **QUIVER** Smack   49ft.5" x 14ft.4" x 7ft.2"
     Bideford, 1852   Signal Hoist: 16.22m. x 4.70 x 2.33
     Official Number: 26710   NRT: 34
First Owner: H. STEVENS, Bideford   Registered: Bideford
Owner: 1871-83, William LAMPREY, Braunton   Registered: Barnstaple

Owner: 1884-94, George LAMPREY, Braunton   Registered: Barnstaple
Owner: 1894, William LAMPREY, Braunton   Registered: Barnstaple
Broken up 1901

Built: Thomas Waters   **RAINBOW** Sloop
     Bideford, 1860   Signal Hoist: PVFW
     Official Number: 28140   NRT: 42
First Owner: J. BALSDON, Bideford   Registered: Bideford
     1865 Lengthened at Bideford and continued in the same ownership.
Second Owner: 1870, G. & J. BELBEN   Registered: Poole
Third Owner: 1880-91, Thomas BELBEN   Registered: Poole
Fourth Owner: 1906-16, Silas F. JENKINS, Vernon's Lane, Appledore
     Registered: Bideford
Fifth Owner: 1920, John HOOPER, Alpha Place, Appledore   Registered: Bideford
Sixth Owner: 1921, W STEVENS, Braunton   Registered: Bideford
     1923 - Went ashore and was broken up at Lynmouth.

241. "Rainbow" proceeds to sea – Mark Myers

Built: C. Raymond **REINE DE PROVOYANCE** Schooner 85.0ft.x22.7x10.2
     St. Irene, France, 1867   Signal Hoist: KCPQ   27.89m. x 7.45 x 3.35
     Official Number: 55889   NRT: 67
Owners: 1918, George CHUGG, 32/64 and Stephen CHUGG, 32/64, of Braunton
     Registered: Barnstaple
Destroyed by fire in the Solent 28 August 1920 and condemned as a total wreck on 20 October 1920

Built: Paul Rogers   **RESULT**   Steel Schooner   102.0ft. 21.7 x 9.1
    Carrickfergus, 1893   Signal Hoist: MQSG   33.46m. x 7.12 x 2.98
    Official Number: 99937   NRT: 88

First Owner: Thomas Ashburner & Co., Church Street, Barrow   Registered: Barrow
Second Owner: 1909, H. S. G. CLARKE, East Hill, Braunton   Registered: Barrow
Third Owners: 1910 shares split between H S G CLARKE, Sidney INCLEDON
        (Master), Frederick INCLEDON, Susan INCLEDON, Mary Ann YEO,
        Thomas Clarke WELCH, and Thomas DUNN all of Braunton.

March 1914 square topsails and yards removed and she was fitted with a 45 b.h.p. single cylinder Kromhaut auxiliary engine.

Fourth Owners: 1914, Henry S. G. CLARKE, Sidney INCLEDON,
        Thomas WELCH   Registered: Barnstaple

Requisitioned by Admiralty for use as a Q-ship in 1917 and renamed HMS Q23, being refitted in January at Lowestoft. She was successful in two actions with submarines but was returned to civilian use in August 1917.

Fifth Owners: 1934, George G. CLARKE and Thomas WELCH Registered: Barnstaple
Sixth Owner: 1939, Thomas WELCH   Registered: Barnstaple
Seventh Owner: 1946, Peter WELCH   Registered: Barnstaple
        1946 – 146hp. Motor installed

1950, participated as FLASH in the film "Outcast of the Isles"

Capt. Welch continued to trade mainly along the South coast and to the Channel Islands and the French Channel ports. Eventually, to ease cargo loading, the mainmast was removed in 1953, and she became a ketch-rigged motorship. By 1967 however there was little cargo available to keep the ship in work, and Capt. Welch decided to convert her hold into passenger accommodation, in the hope of gaining charter work. The refit was still incomplete when he died aboard his ship at Jersey in the same year.

Eighth Owner: 1967, Mrs. Peter WELCH   Registered: Barnstaple

The *Result* was sailed to Exeter and was laid up in the city basin, a forlorn sight with the traditional blue band of mourning painted around her hull. Her working life had ended after seventy-four years, but the Exeter Maritime Museum continued to care for her and three years later Mrs. Welch sold her to the Ulster Folk and Transport Museum. The schooner sailed from Exeter on the 4th October 1970 for Brixham, where she was surveyed, and then sailed, on her final voyage, for Belfast.

Ninth Owner: 1970, Cultra Maritime Museum, Belfast   Register: Closed

The Museum commissioned the Harland & Wolff shipyard to carry out some restoration work. In 1979 the hull was lifted from the water and transported to a dry-land site at the Museum at Cultra, Co. Down. The Museum's intention was to restore her to her original form as a three-masted schooner, but in the succeeding years little if any further work has been done, the cost being too great for the Museum's resources and the remains of the vessel are a sad sight at this time.

242. The "Result" at Ilfracombe in 1952 – Peter Welch
For further illustrations see the chapter on the "Result"

Built: Watson & Fox   **ROSETTA**   Ketch   76.3ft. x 19.5 x 8.7
      Plymouth, 1890   Signal Hoist: QFJH   25.03m. x 6.40 x 2.85
      Official Number: 97468   NRT: 57
First Owners: John RICE, Cattedown, Plymouth   Registered: Plymouth
Second Owner: 1907, Stephen S. CHUGG, Braunton   Registered: Plymouth
Third Owners: 1916, Stephen G. B. CHUGG 32/64,
                  Ruth CHUGG 32/64   Registered: Barnstaple
                  1916, refitted and altered
Fourth Owner: 1920, Stanley R. WOOD, Clonakilty, Co. Cork Registered: Barnstaple
Fifth Owner: 1922, Ludwig K. ANDERSEN, Harbour House, Portmadoc
                                                          Registered: Aberystwyth
1934 still listed under the ownership of L. K. Andersen.
   She became a constructive total loss in 1944, after stranding at Barry, at which time she is understood to have been under Irish ownership.

*243. "Rosetta" when newly purchased by Stephen Chugg about 1907.
Braunton Museum*

244. "Rosetta", proceeding under auxiliary motor – Appledore Museum

202

245. Rosetta" lying at Bude, 8 June 1940 - Appledore Museum

Built: Robert Cock **ROSIE** Ketch 83.0ft. x 21.0 x 9.9
Appledore, 1885 Signal Hoist: KCVO 27.23m. x 6.89 x 3.25
Official Number: 79358 NRT 68
First Owner: Robert Cock, Appledore Registered: Bideford
Second Owner: 1898, Griffith Edwin DEDWITH, Portmadoc Registered: Bideford
Third Owner: 1914, Edward MAYNARD, Bude, Registered: Bideford
Fourth Owner: 1920, Mary A. Beddis, New Ferry, Cheshire Registered: Bideford
1920 - Auxiliary engine fitted.
Sixth Owner: 1934, Lewis WILLIAMS, Oakly Cottage, Portmadoc
Registered: Bideford

George HARTNOLL of Braunton appears to have had an interest in this vessel which was engaged in the Newfoundland trade in her early years.
Eventually foundered and was hulked on the Pembrokeshire coast.

Built: Massey **SAINT AUSTELL** Ketch 74.0ft. x 19.2 x 9.3
Portreath, St. Austell, 1873 Signal Hoist: WSLG 24.28m. x 6.30 x 3.05
Official Number: 69841 NRT: 47
First Owner: T HITCHENS & Co., Fowey Registered: Fowey
Owner: 1884-91: Thomas HITCHINS jr, St. Austell Registered: Fowey
Owner: 1906, William BENNETT, Tywardreath Registered: Fowey
Owner: 1912, Samuel Guard, Appledore Registered: Fowey
Owner: 1913, Samuel Guard, Appledore Registered: Bideford
10 February, 1916 on passage from Cardiff to Barnstaple with coal under Captain Guard she stranded on Half-Tide Rock off Castle Point, Carlingford and was declared a total loss. The wreck was purchased by Braunton men and rebuilt
1917: Repaired at Appledore Signal Hoist: JSCD
1917, Henry S. G. CLARKE, Thomas WELCH, Peter STRIBLING,
of Braunton Registered: Barnstaple
Owner: 1934, Robert Nicholson, Kilkeel, Co. Down Registered: Barnstaple
Owner: 1949/1951 Under Appledore owners, she was sold out of trade in 1951, and later sank following a fire off Wicklow in 1952.

246. The auxiliary ketch "Saint Austell" at Avonmouth Old Docks. Bill Mitchell

247. The "Saint Austell" alongside Appledore Quay at high tide. Bill Mitchell

248. The three crew of the "Saint Austell," complete with four dogs!
Appledore Museum

249. High and dry! But after being declared a constructive total loss she was purchased by Braunton owners and repaired at Appledore. The "St Austell" aground on the Half Tide Rock at Carlingford Lough, 18 February 1916.
Appledore Musem.

250. The ketch "Saltash", previously the "Iron King" and before that the "Desmond" under which name the entry for this vessel appears. - Mark Myers

SARAH ANN   Ketch/trow   55ft. x 16.6 x 8.1

Built: Newport, Mon., 1858   Signal Hoist: MDPH   18.04m. x 5.45 x 2.66
Official Number: 16940   NRT: 58
First Owner: H. OAKLEY, Newport, Mon.   Registered: Newport.Mon
Owner: 1884: James TUCKER, Mrs G TUCKER, Marwood, Braunton
                                                    Registered: Newport, Mon
Owner: 1889, Bernard TUCKER, Cross Tree Farm, Braunton
                                                    Registered: Newport, Mon
Owner: 1891, Miss E. D. TUCKER, South Street, Braunton Registered: Newport, Mon
                Not listed after 1900

SHAMROCK   Ketch   74.0ft. x 18.0 x 9.0

Built: Abbott, Hull, 1863   Signal Hoist: VMRT   24.28m. x 5.90 x 2.95
Official Number   NRT: 77
First Owner: R. GILLAN   Registered: Middlesbrough
Owner: 1884, Joseph JEWETT, Goole   Registered: Middlesbrough
Owner: 1886, Joseph JEWITT, Southampton   Registered: Middlesbrough
Owner: 1891-1910: Mrs Sarah Elizabeth LEMON, Newport Road, Barnstaple
        and W. WILLIAMS of Braunton   Registered: Middlesbrough
1911 The vessel was buried in a breached sea wall at Horsey Island as a part of the remedial work to close the breach.

SIR FRANCIS DRAKE   Smack   61.9ft. a 17.4 x 7.7

Built: William Westacott, Barnstaple, 1867   Signal Hoist: None   20.31m. x 5.71 x 2.53
Official Number: 58361   NRT: 45
First Owner: Francis DRAKE, 32/64, Robert DRAKE, 32/64, Braunton
                                                    Registered: Barnstaple
Second Owner: 1883-91, James MILL, Appledore   Registered: Barnstaple
January, 1900, the vessel was lost off Nash Point, Glamorgan whilst bound from Appledore to Bristol with a cargo of gravel under Captain J. H. Scilly and a crew of two. She foundered and was lost offshore in a southerly gale, wind force 9.

STRANGER   Sloop   54.5ft. x 17.4 x 7.5

Built: John Goss, Pilton, Barnstaple, 1862   Signal Hoist: None   17.88m. x 5.71 x 2.46
Official Number: 29673   NRT: 41
First Owner: Thomas DULLING   Registered: Barnstaple
Second Owner: 1884, Thomas DULLING Jr. Barnstaple   Registered: Barnstaple
                Re-rigged as a Smack
                Later converted to a ketch
Third Owner: 1901, Mary CLARKE, 32/64 George MITCHELL (master)
                and MANLEY All of Braunton   Registered: Barnstaple
Fourth Owner: 1905-21, William DALLING, Rolles Quay, Barnstaple
                                                    Registered: Barnstaple
            Not listed in Mercantile Navy List 1934

STRATHISLA   Ketch   69.2ft. x 19.2 x 9.3

Built: John Duncan, Garmouth, 1860   Signal Hoist: PRFS   22.70m. x 6.30 x 3.05
Official Number: 27417   NRT: 71
First Owner: FORSYTH & Co., Banff   Registered: Banff

Second Owner: 1881, George CHUGG, South Street, Braunton. H.S.G. CLARKE, STRIBLING and SCOINS of Braunton also held shares.

Registered: Barnstaple

At the time of her loss George CHUGG held 64/64.

On 23 September 1886 on passage from Kinsale to Newport, Mon. in ballast under Captain G. Millman, whilst attempting to enter the river Taw in a fog and without a pilot, she struck on the North Ridge. The impact brought down the main gaff, which smashed the steering wheel and this added to a bad leak and choked pumps, caused the crew of 4 to abandon the vessel, which drifted away on the rising tide, striking the rocks to the east of the lighthouse and later the rocks on Kilstone Point.

Built: Charles Gent **SULTAN** Ketch 70.6ft. 17.3 x 7.2
Plymouth, 1864 Signal Hoist: WBCG 23.16m. x 5.67 x 2.36
Official Number: 48963 NRT: 51
Owner: 1875, John CLARKE, Ann CLARK, Charles CLARKE, Len CHUGG
and Charles MITCHELL of Braunton. Registered: Barnstaple
Owner: 1883-91, Philip ELLIS, Oreston, Plymouth Registered: Plymouth
Owner: 1906, Mrs. Ann CLARKE, Wrafton, Braunton Registered: Barnstaple
Owner: 1912: Claude L. CHUGG, Braunton Registered: Barnstaple
Owner: 1914, Charles L CHUGG, Braunton Registered: Barnstaple
Owner: 1920, Charles M. CLARKE, Braunton Registered: Barnstaple

Broken up 1925

Built: Massey **T.M.P.** Ketch 63.2ft. x 18.3 x 7.8
Portreath, Cornwall, 1874 Signal Hoist: TVDF 20.73m. x 6.00 x 2.56
Official Number: 68862 NRT: 50
Owner: 1883, Martin F. PAGE, Blakeney Registered: Kings Lynn
Owner: 1888-1891, Edward C. TURNER, Blakeney Registered: Lynn
Owner: 1897, Sidney John INCLEDON 32/64, Grace Ann INCLEDON, 32/64
Registered: Barnstaple
Owner: 1909, Henry S. G. CLARKE, Braunton Registered: Barnstaple
Owner: 1916, Dr. Robert Eliston WRIGHT Registered: Barnstaple

12 February 1917, stranded on rocks 1 mile west of Ilfracombe on passage from Barnstaple to Newport, Mon. with a cargo of gravel with a crew of three. She became a total loss.

Built: William Westacott **TELEGRAPH** Ketch 41.0ft. x 19.1 x 7.7
Barnstaple, 1869 Signal Hoist: None 13.45m. x 6.27 x 2.53
Official Number: 62971 NRT: 41
Owner: 1884, William STOATE, Watchet Registered: Bridgwater
Owner: 1886-91, John STOATE, Watchet Registered: Bridgwater
Owner: 1906-12, James STOATE, Watchet Registered: Bridgwater
Owner: 1913, Walter J. WEBBER, Quay Street, Minehead Registered: Bridgwater
Owner: 1920, Thomas WATTS, Braunton Registered: Barnstaple
Owner: 1925, W. STOKES, Weston-Super-Mare Registered: Barnstaple

Foundered in St. George's Channel, 1926

Built:	**THADDEUS** Sloop	40.6ft. x 12.5 x 7.8
    Poole, 1814	Signal Hoist: None	13.32m. x 4.10 x 2.56
    Official Number:		NRT:
Owner: 1818,		Registered: Ilfracombe
Owner: 1822, Thomas WESTREN, yeoman 48/64, William HOW, cordwainer
       16/64, master George JONES, of Braunton	Registered: Barnstaple
    Wrecked on Croyde beach 2 August 1827, possibly carrying coal.

Built: William Clibbert	**THOMAS** Ketch	68.2ft. x 16.2 x 7.3
    Appledore, 1857	Signal Hoist: MRHF	22.37m. x 5.31 x 2.39
    Official Number: 19279		NRT: 40
First Owner: 1857-1870 at least, W. SCANTLEBURY, Fowey	Registered: Fowey
Owner: 1884, Clifford SYMONS, Bridgwater	Registered: Bridgwater
Owner: 1888, COLHURST SYMONS & Co, Bridgwater	Registered: Bridgwater
Owner: 1890, James WHITE, Heanton, James ISAAC, butcher Braunton
	Registered: Barnstaple
Owner: 1896, James Isaac 32/64, Alice THORNE 32/64	Registered: Barnstaple
Owner: 1897-1920, William LEONARD, New Street, Bideford	Registered: Barnstaple
    Broken up, 1925

Built:	**THREE BROTHERS** Ketch	48.0ft. x 17.3 x 7.3
    Llanelly, 1827	Signal Hoist: None	15.75m. x 5.67 x 2.39
    Official Number: 15518		NRT: 32
Owner: 1850-57, SHOPLAND & Co.	Registered: Bideford
Owner: 1857, Barnstaple Owners	Registered: Barnstaple
Owner: 1865, Francis DRAKE Sr. 64/64, Heanton Punchardon, Braunton
	Registered: Barnstaple
Owner: 1866, Francis DRAKE, jr. 64/64, Braunton	Registered: Barnstaple
Owner: 1867, Thomas HARLYN, Appledore	Registered: Barnstaple
On 20 July 1879 on passage from Appledore to Newport, Mon. the wind fell light and she went ashore on Croyde Rocks, later drifting onto Braunton Sands. Captain Thomas Harlyn and her other crew member put off in the ship's boat but despite the efforts of the Northam Burrows Lifeboat, MARY ANN (II), the men were never found.

Built	**THOMASIN & MARY** Ketch
    Boscastle, 1855	Signal Hoist: MRCQ
    Official Number: 19226		NRT: 49
Owner: 1884-1914, Llewellin HOLE, Watchet	Registered: Bridgwater
Owner: 1920, William J. LAMEY, Myrtle Street, Appledore	Registered: Bridgwater
Owner: 1923, SCOBLING, Braunton	Registered: Bridgwater
    1924, Lost in Walton Bay, Portishead on passage to Hayle

Built:	**TRALY** Ketch	79.7ft. x 20.0 x 9.0
    Millwall, London, 1912	Signal Hoist: JRDM	26.15m. x 6.45 x 2.95
    Official Number: 128846		NRT: 55
    Built with a fully powered 70h.p. engine using sails as an auxiliary.
First Owner: Robert McCOWAN & SONS LTD, Denny Street, Tralee
	Registered: Tralee
Second Owner: 1919, The WYNFIELD SHIPPNG Co Ltd, Grimsby

                        (Thomas E. DOWNEY mgr.)   Registered: Tralee
Third Owner: 1923, John CLARKE, Bay View, Braunton and
                 George CLARKE, Hills View, Braunton   Registered: Barnstaple
Fourth Owner: 1937, W. W. PETHERICK, (A. PETHERICK mgr.), Bude
                                                         Registered: Barnstaple
She was purchased to replace the Bude ketch *CERES* which had been lost in Bideford Bay. Probably broken up in 1989, she remained in Danish hands after he sale overseas in 1958.

251. The "Traly" on her first trip to Bude for her new owners in 1937
Bill Mitchell

252. The "Traly" entering Bude
Braunton Museum

210

253. "Traly" on the blocks for her annual maintenance.

211

254. *"Traly" at Rolle Quay, Barnstaple, in 1939 – Braunton Museum*

Built: Thomas Waters   **TRIO**   Ketch   52.5ft. x 16.5 x 7.6
    Bideford, 1861   Signal Hoist: QHJF   17.22m. x 5.41 x 2.49
    Official Number: 298939   NRT: 38
First Owner: Thomas. WATTS, Braunton   Registered: Bideford
Second Owner: 1876-1895, Thomas STEVENS, Braunton   Registered: Bideford
Third Owner: 1896-1920, Henry W. LESLIE, Meeting Street, Appledore
                                                                                                          Registered: Bideford
                                Hulk broken up 1950

255. The ketch "Trio" seen at Ilfracombe in 1897 - David Clement Collection

213

Built: Thomas Waters   **TWO SISTERS** Brigantine   70.0ft. x 19.0 x 9.4
     Bideford, 1865   Signal Hoist: None   22.96m. x 6.23 x 3.08
     Official Number: 47889   NRT: 62
First Owner: CHUGG & Co., Braunton   Registered: Bideford
Second Owner: 1884-91, John CHUGG, Mary Grace CHUGG, Kitty Ann
     CHUGG, Heanton Punchardon, Braunton   Registered: Barnstaple
Third Owner: 1905-35, Philip Kelly HARRIS, Appledore   Registered: Barnstaple
     During this period she was re-rigged as a ketch.

She took the last cargo of manganese ore from Velator Quay about 1900. This was mined at Spreacombe Mine, Braunton from the 1870s and taken to Big Quay by horse and cart. *"Two Sisters"* was sold out of trade in 1939.

256. The ketch "Two Sisters" - Mark Myers

257. The "Two Sisters" in the Richmond Dry Dock at Appledore
Appledore Museum

Built: Dyer   **ULELIA** Schooner   75.4ft. x 19.9 x 9.4
     Truro, 1898   Signal Hoist: RBKM   24.74m. x 6.53 x 3.08
     Official Number: 74429   NRT: 58
First Owner: John ESTLICK   Registered: Barnstaple
Second Owner: 1898, Gavin McF. HOPE   Registered: Bideford
Third Owner: 1899, William Kingdon SLADE, Appledore   Registered: Barnstaple
Fourth Owner: 1901, William DRAKE, William ESTLICK, Braunton
                                                       Registered: Barnstaple
                         1901, reduced to a ketch
Fifth Owner: 1906-14, Wm. K. SLADE 32/64, George QUANCE 32/64
                                                         Registered: Barnstaple
Sixth Owner: 1915, Mrs. TAYLOR   Registered: Bideford
Seventh Owner: 1916-20, Josephine HOBBS, Appledore   Registered: Bideford
Eighth Owner: 1921, John HUTCHINGS and Percy HARRIS Registered: Bideford
     1930, missed stays on entering Rhoscarberry, Ireland and was wrecked on the adjacent rocks.

Built: John Stephens   **VICTORIA** Sloop   52.0ft. x 15.4 x 7.4
     Port Gavern, Padstow, 1853   Signal Hoist: MLQB   17.06m. x 10.65 x 2.43
     Official Number: 18391   NRT: 40
First Owners: Carter & Co.   Registered: Padstow
Second Owners, 1888-1907, Thomas CLARKE, Wrafton, Braunton
                                                        Registered: Barnstaple
                    1890 – Re-rigged as a ketch
                        1907, Broken up

Built: **VISION** Ketch
Owned by CLARKE Braunton, and went missing on passage from Appledore to Ireland. Charlie HARRIS and crew were from Appledore, but no other details provided to identify this vessel.

Built: **VIXEN** Ketch
     Newquay, 1889   Signal Hoist: QNMB
     Official Number: 62777   NRT: 44
Owner: 1889-1914, Henry ROUSE, Lerryn, Cornwall   Registered: Padstow
                1906 – NRT reduced to 35
Owner: 1920, George IRWIN, Cranleigh Terrace, Combe Martin   Registered: Padstow
Owner 1921: R CHICHESTER, Braunton   Registered: Barnstaple
Owner: 1934, Thomas H BLENCH, Simonside, Heaton, Newcastle
                                                       Registered: Barnstaple

Built: **WATER LILY** 2 m schooner   86.2ft. x 21.5 x 10.3
     Banff, 1876   Signal Hoist: None   28.28m. x 7.05 x 3.38
     Official Number: 70521   NRT: 85
First Owner: 1876-1884 Donald GEORGESON, Wick   Registered: Wick
Second Owner: 1885-95, John HOWARD, Top Locks, Runcorn Registered: Liverpool
Third Owner: 1906, Timothy DRISCOLL, Sherkin Island, Co. Cork
                                                       Registered: Liverpool
Fourth Owner: 1910, Harry C. CHUGG, Church Street, Braunton

                                                            Registered: Liverpool
Fifth Owner: 1913, George CHUGG 32/64, Henry Cecil CHUGG 32/64
                                                            Registered: Barnstaple
On 10 September 1917 she was sunk by German U-boat 8 miles north by east of Pendeen lighthouse on passage from Runcorn for Cherbourg laden with coal.

Built: Evans & Cox   **WESLEYANA** Smack   52.0ft. x 13.9 x 6.0
    Cleavehouses, Bideford, 1842 Signal Hoist: None   17.06m. x 4.56 x 1.97
    Official Number: 5528   NRT: 25
Owner: 1882   Registered: Bideford
19 September 1882, Stranded on the beach at Tintagel while loading slate stone destined for Penzance and was a constructive total loss. Wrecked as a dandy, when salvaged she was later rebuilt as a ketch.
Owner: 1882-4, William TRICK, Appledore   Registered: Bideford
Owner: 1888-92, William LEMON, Barnstaple   Registered: Bideford
Owner: 1894, G. BUTLER, Braunton   Registered: Bideford
                1895, Foundered off Lynmouth

Built: Thomas Waters   **WHY NOT** Sloop   50.6ft. x 16.5 x 7.2
    Bideford, 1851   Signal Hoist: LJQK   16.60m. x 5.41 x 2.36
    Official Number: 13837   NRT: 34
First Owner: FERNANDES & Co.   Registered: Bideford
Owner: 1860, J. STROUT   Registered: Bideford
Owner: 1861, Mary HEDDON, Thomas WHITE, James WHITE, Braunton
                                                     Registered: Barnstaple
Owner: 1884-91, Robert COCK, Appledore   Registered: Barnstaple
Owner: 1906, James H. COCK, Appledore   Registered: Barnstaple
                Not listed in Mercantile Navy List 1910

Built: **WILLIAM & CATHERINE** Sloop   44.0ft
    1791   Signal Hoist: None   14.43m.
    Official Number: NRT: 30
Owner: 1857,   Registered: Ilfracombe
                        Lost 1864

Built: Clements   **WILLIAM MARTYN** Schooner   87.1ft. x 22.2 x 10.4
    Gannel River, Newquay, 1873 Signal Hoist: SWQL   28.58m. x 7.28 x 3.41
    Official Number: 69455   NRT: 82
First Owner   1873-89, John Crocker, Newquay   Registered: Padstow
Second Owner: 1890, John ENNOR, Newquay   Registered: Padstow
Third Owner: 1906, James KEARNS, Arklow   Registered: Dublin
Fourth Owner: 1915, W. CORNEY, and A. CORNEY, Braunton
                                                     Registered: Barnstaple
16 March 1917, whilst bound from Newport to Cork with coal she was sunk by German U-boat 9 miles west by ½W of Ram Head, Youghal (10 miles south-east of Youghal.) The submarine commander took the Certificate of Registry when departing.

Built: W. S. Kelly   **WOODCOCK** Steel Ketch 61.3ft. x 17.7 x 6.7
    Plymouth, 1895   Signal Hoist: MQTG   20.11m. x 5.81 x 2.20
    Official Number: 105768   NRT: 30
First Owner: G. HARKER & Co.   Registered: London
Second: Owner: 1903-14, David Evans DERBY, Saundersfoot Registered: Milford
Third Owner: 1920, Thomas BASSETT, Lower Down, Braunton
       Registered: Milford
   Refitted 1921 as a fully powered motor vessel with auxiliary sails
Fourth Owner: 1934, George CHUGG and Cecil CHUGG Braunton
       Registered: Barnstaple
Lost 23 December 1943, 1.25 miles north-north-east of Hangman Hill, in Combe Martin Bay

258. "Woodcock" at Ilfracombe in 1930 with Captain George Chugg.
The mate at the time was G. Rawlstone.
Courtesy Roger Chugg

259. Ketch "Woodcock" at Velator in 1936 – Braunton Museum

260. "Woodcock" discharging at Bude – Bill Mitchell

Built: Bevans   **YEO**   Ketch   56.4ft. x 18.0 x 7.5
     Llanelly, 1862   Signal Hoist: None   18.50m. x 5.90 x 2.46
     Official Number: 29402   NRT: 43
First Owner: KIRKWOOD   Registered: Llanelly
Second Owner: 1866, R. WREY   Registered: Bideford
                       Damage repaired 1869
Third Owner   1869-1885, Richard Blake PEARSE (Sr.) Barnstaple
                                                        Registered: Barnstaple
Fourth Owner: 1886, Richard Blake PEARSE, (jr) Portland St, Exeter
                                                        Registered: Barnstaple
Fifth Owner: 1888 -1891, Philip C. LAMEY, Croyde, Braunton
                                                        Registered: Barnstaple
Sixth Owner: 1895, T. BUTLER, Packwood, Braunton and
                     Thomas LEMON, Barnstaple.   Registered: Barnstaple
Seventh Owner: 1900-1906, William LEMON, Newport Rd, Barnstaple
                                                        Registered: Barnstaple
Eighth Owner: 1910-15, John LIGHT, Trinity Street, Barnstaple
                                                        Registered: Barnstaple
     1915 Lost off Ilfracombe in heavy weather, whilst on passage from Lydney to
                                     Barnstaple with coal.

261. The ketch "Yeo" at Blue Weir, September 1903. - Braunton Museum
The men have just completed throwing the ballast over the side to enable the vessel to float on the tide. Those we see from left to right are: Fred and Aubrey Manaton (standing); T. Phillips, J. Mullen, R. Mullen, J. Mitchell, J. Lamprey, B. Tucker, and J. Woolacott who is seated in front.

262. The crew of the "Yeo" pose at the bows for their photograph shortly before she was lost in 1915. They are W. Packwood, Harry Stevens and Jack White
– Mark Myers

THE GRAVEL BARGES

As mentioned previously those vessels used exclusively within the Bar on the estuaries of the Taw and Torridge were not required to be formally registered with the Board of Trade, and as a result full details are harder to come by. However a brief list of known Braunton barges is appended below, of which the *"Hilda"* is dealt with more extensively in the general schedule as being the last gravel barge to work under sail.

Barge	Principal Owner
Dabchick	J. Mitchell
Discovery	C. Chugg
Duck	J. Lane
Hilda	H. Mitchell
Ironing Box	W. Darracott
Lena	C. Chugg
Lifeboat	J. Paddison
Rowena	J. Incledon
S.P.E.C.	W. Mullen

ADDENDUM

The following vessels have also been discovered which are suggested to have had links with Braunton, but no direct connection has been unearthed. These connections could be share ownership, or vessels being manned by men from Braunton and the immediate district around, including Wrafton, Heanton and Velator. Any information that could clarify the association would be appreciated by Braunton Museum.

Built: 1837   **ALEXANDER** Smack   49.7ft.
                     Signal Hoist: None   15.12m.
                     Wrecked 1859   NRT: 41

Built: 1746   **BETSY** Sloop   42.11ft.
                     Signal Hoist: None   13.11m.
                                                         NRT: 35
Wrecked on passage Caen to Appledore in ballast, 1828.

Built: Thomas Green   **BILLOW** Brig   62.4ft. x 19.4 x 10.5
     Appledore, 1837   Signal Hoist: None   19.02m. x 5.91 x 3.20
                                                                         NRT: 84
Owner: Captain Fishwick & Co.   Registered: Newport
Lengthened 1849 and converted to schooner rig.

Built: William Westcott, **HARLEQUIN** 2-m schooner 84.6ft. x 22.1 x 7.8
       Barnstaple, 1879   Signal Hoist: None   25.79m. x 6.74 x 2.38
Official Number: 80209   NRT: 85
First Owner: R. Heard   Registered: Bideford
Second Owner: Kinsale Shipping Co.   Registered: Kinsale
Lost 24 October 1896 when sunk in collision with steamer *"Ouse"* in Barry Roads. Crew of 4 saved.

Built: George Crocker   **INSTOW**   Smack   42.5ft.
       Bideford, 1820   Signal Hoist: None   12.95m.
                                                                   NRT: 27

Lengthened 1836 and rigged as a sloop

Built: William Waters,   **JOHN BLACKWELL** 2m schr 64.1ft. x 18.3 x 9.5
       Sea Locks, Bideford, 1862   Signal Hoist: 19.54m. x 5.58 x 2.89
Official Number: NRT: 65
First Owner: Rolle Canal Co.   Registered: Bideford
First Master: Captain N. Collin
Second Master: William Jewell (1864) of Clovelly
Used in the trade to Lisbon and the Mediterranean she is understood to have been manned by the following Braunton men from Velator:
    George Butler, Mate; Dick Bedford, seaman; and Charles Pedrick, cook
      (See illustration in *Chapter 8 Pierhead Paintings*.)
                The vessel was lost in 1867.

Built: 1881   **LUCY OF DUNDALK** Ketch
Official Number: 76254   Signal Hoist: None   NRT: 52
Owner: C. D. King, Annagasson
Captain George Welch of Braunton is believed to have been master at one time.
Not listed MNL 1883

Built: George Crocker   **MARY ANN**   Sloop
       Bidefore, 1826   Signal Hoist: None   NRT: 61
Owner: 1837, Thomas Green, Appledore

Built: William Clibbett   **SAINT BRANNOCK** Schooner 57.5ft.
       Appledore, 1838   Signal Hoist: None   17.53m.
                                                                 NRT: 82
First Owner: Harris & Co.
Lengthened 1863 Appledore

Built: Thomas Green   **SERAPHINA**   Smack   45.4ft.
       Appledore, 1839   Signal Hoist: MRDN   13.84m.
Official Number: 19239   NRT: 38
Owner (1874) George Parkhouse, Appledore   Registered: Bideford

Built: W. R. Guy   **TELEGRAPH** Schooner   55.2ft. x 18.0 x 8.3
    Porth Gaverne, 1859   Signal Hoist: None   16.82m. x 5.48 x 2.54
Official Number: 27271   NRT: 36
Owned to 1906, Warwick R. Guy, Port Isaac, Cornwall   Registered: Padstow
Final Owner: Mary Ann Lang   Registered: Padstow
Swept by tide onto Monkey Island in river Taw whilst carrying cargo of coal from Cardiff to Fremington and became a total loss on 27 December 1906.

Built: Cei bach   **VENUS** Sloop   41.6ft.
    Cardigan, 1820   Signal Hoist: None   12.68m.
         NRT: 26
Wrecked on the Welsh coast 1865